PRAISE FOR *WHAT'S WRONG WITH OUR SCHOOLS*

"A clear, fluent, and (yes!) commonsense alternative to the culture of romantic progressivism that has captured so completely the education establishment throughout North America. The authors have read the research, but they draw also critically on classroom experience and make recommendations that are practical in the distinctly unideal reality of today's public school systems."
—**Peter Brimelow,** author of *The Worm in the Apple*

"This is simply the best book on the public school I have seen. Written in straightforwa~~~ ~~~~~~~, parents are informed about the foolish fads that still afflict ou~~~~~~~~~~~~~~~~~~~~~~~~~~~~~~~~ ~~ch and without condescension, ~ ~~~~~~~~~~~~~~~~~~~~~~~~~~~~~." —**Mark Holmes,** assistant dir~~~~~~~~~~~~~~~~~~~~~~~~~ oronto–OISE, Graduate School ~~~~~~~~~~~~~~~~~~~~~~~~~ *rmation of Canada's Schools*

"The au~~~~~~~~~~~~~~~~~~~~~~~~~~~~~~~~~~ rogressive educati~~~~~~~~~~~~~~~~~~~~~~~~~~~~~ shion why much ~~~~~~~~~~~~~~~~~~~~~~~~~~~~~~~ decades. Whole~~~~~~~~~~~~~~~~~~~~~~~~~~~~~~~~ are nicely critiqu~~~~~~~~~~~~~~~~~~~~~~~~~~~~ culprit in all this~~~~~~~~~~~~~~~~~~~~~~~~~~~~~ ninate the profes~~~~~~~~~~~~~~~~~~~~~~~~~~~~ g whether the en~~~~~~~~~~~~~~~~~~~~~~~~~~~~ ators' Distingui~~~~~~~~~~~~~~~~~~~~~~~~~~ issouri–St. Louis~

What's Wrong with Our Schools

and How We Can Fix Them

MICHAEL C. ZWAAGSTRA,
RODNEY A. CLIFTON,
AND JOHN C. LONG

ROWMAN & LITTLEFIELD EDUCATION
A division of
ROWMAN & LITTLEFIELD PUBLISHERS, INC.
Lanham • New York • Toronto • Plymouth, UK

Published by Rowman & Littlefield Education
A division of Rowman & Littlefield Publishers, Inc.
A wholly owned subsidiary of The Rowman & Littlefield Publishing Group, Inc.
4501 Forbes Boulevard, Suite 200, Lanham, Maryland 20706
http://www.rowmaneducation.com

Estover Road, Plymouth PL6 7PY, United Kingdom

British Library Cataloguing in Publication Information Available

Library of Congress Cataloging-in-Publication Data

Zwaagstra, Michael C.
    What's wrong with our schools : and how we can fix them / Michael C. Zwaagstra, Rodney A. Clifton, and John C. Long.
        p. cm.
    Includes bibliographical references.
    ISBN 978-1-60709-157-8 (cloth : alk. paper) — ISBN 978-1-60709-158-5 (pbk. : alk. paper) — ISBN 978-1-60709-159-2 (electronic)
    1. Public schools—United States. 2. Public schools—Canada. 3. Educational change—United States. 4. Educational change—Canada. I. Clifton, Rodney A., 1944– II. Long, John C. III. Title.
    LA217.2.Z93 2010
    370.973—dc22   2010007834

∞™ The paper used in this publication meets the minimum requirements of American National Standard for Information Sciences—Permanence of Paper for Printed Library Materials, ANSI/NISO Z39.48-1992.

Printed in the United States of America

In your light we see light. (Psalm 36:9)

To our teachers who passed the light to us, and to our students who passed the light to others.

To all teachers who need the light, and to all students who need enlightened teachers.

Contents

Acknowledgments

The American writer William Zinsser truthfully claims that the craft of writing and doing it well is hard thinking and careful rewriting. We agree, and we need to thank a number of critical readers who have helped us with our thinking, writing, and rewriting. First, we wish to thank two of our academic colleagues, now retired, for their challenging and insightful criticisms and helpful suggestions. Mark Holmes and Michael J. B. Jackson are two of the best colleagues any group of authors could possibly have. They were tough-minded but relentlessly constructive, generous with their time and talents, giving us many suggestions that we know improved the book. We benefited immeasurably from their knowledge of the educational literature and the administration of schools; but especially we benefited from their common sense. Michael J. B. Jackson read two drafts of the manuscript, and we are very grateful for his insights and criticisms on both occasions.

We also had a group of parents, teachers, and administrators, who have dealt with many of the issues in the book, read a penultimate draft of the manuscript. These colleagues provided both corrections and suggestions. To Edwin Buettner, Jerome Cranston, Malkin Dare, Simone Kirwan, Lyle Lorenz, Chantel McIntyre, Dave Poersch, Laura Reimer, Robert Renaud, and Dorothy Young we thank you for your assistance and advice. You have helped us write a better book.

Finally, our families put up with the countless hours we spent working on this book. Our wives, Angela Zwaagstra, Elaine Clifton, and Deloris Long, graciously permitted us the time we needed to complete the work. Their love and support made it possible. Thank you very much.

Even though we are grateful for the assistance and support we received from the people we have acknowledged, we alone are responsible for the contents of the book.

Introduction

Whatever Happened to Common Sense?

Whatever happened to common sense in education? If you are a parent, teacher, principal, or school trustee, perhaps this question has crossed your mind. Perhaps you have even heard the same question, or a similar one, from your children's teachers, your neighbors, or your friends. Whether it is the lack of content in some school curricula, the antitesting ideology promoted by many educators, the no-fail policies that have been enacted by some school boards, or the pervasiveness of what might be described as "edu-speak" or "edu-babble," there is growing concern and skepticism with some of the more recent policies and practices in many public schools in North America.

As three educators with considerable experience, we have noticed with increasing concern how a number of these educational policies and practices have departed from what we consider to be common sense. Often we have been dismayed by what we have observed because it is contrary to our understanding of what is required for effective teaching, learning, and school management.

Michael Zwaagstra is a full-time high school teacher with a master's degree in education and a decade of teaching experience in public schools. Rod Clifton has been a teacher and a university professor for more than three decades, and is a specialist in the sociology of education. John Long, recently retired, was a university professor of educational administration and an award-winning teacher whose teaching and administrative experience at the grade school, college, and university levels extends over four decades.

The fact that we are troubled by some aspects of contemporary public schooling might incline some to label us what E. D. Hirsch Jr. (1996, 231) has called "mavericks" in the field of education. Though we are all educators, we are critical of some of the practices and policies in schools. Nevertheless, each of us has great admiration for the work that teachers and principals perform, and we think that their jobs have become increasingly difficult. Part of this difficulty is the fact that some of these practices have been imposed on teachers and administrators without the benefit of their considered professional judgment.

Often, the professional judgment of teachers and principals reflects the practicality and common sense that emerges in the hustle, bustle, and ambiguities of teaching and administering schools. In our minds, both teachers and school administrators need a significant degree of freedom to teach and manage classrooms and schools without unreasonable interference from senior administrators, school board members, parents, and members of the public. Nevertheless, they must be accountable if they are given this discretion in teaching students and managing schools. In fact, we think that currently there is too little discretion granted to educators and too little accountability as well (Greene 2005).

We know from many sources—reports, research studies, surveys, and numerous conversations that we have had with parents, teachers, school administrators, and school board members—that we are not alone in our concerns. In fact, there is considerable dissatisfaction and frustration with several aspects of the character and operation of public education in North America. Parents, specifically, but many teachers and principals as well, have serious concerns about what they see as guru-inspired bandwagons and inadequately justified school practices.

Sometimes the people who are not educators think that they are not well equipped to challenge the so-called experts when they hear that certain instructional methods are "brain-based" or "research-based," that all students have "individual learning styles," and that "constructivist teaching" requires "authentic assessment." Many parents probably realize that their attempt to talk to educators forces them to struggle with understanding what we call "edu-babble." Given the prevalence of such jargon, it is especially difficult for parents to know what to say or what to do if they want to assist their children who are having difficulty or if their children require more challenging school work.

The fact that an increasing number of parents are choosing alternatives to the traditional public schooling for their children is also evidence of their genuine dissatisfaction (see Burke 2009; Lips, Marshall, and Burke 2008). Almost five thousand charter schools are now operating in more than forty U.S. states and one Canadian province (Alberta) with a total enrollment of almost 1.5 million students. Of course, we realize that charter schools are public schools, but they are structured so that teachers and administrators have greater accountability for the results their students achieve.

Moreover, a number of states in the United States provide scholarships so that poor students can attend private schools and some states provide tax credits to parents for their children's tuition fees. In addition, private agencies, such as Sylvan Learning and Kumon Mathematics and Reading Centers, operate in hundreds of locations across North America, with more centers opening every year. These institutions provide much-needed remedial tutoring for thousands of students. We wonder why parents need to pay for remedial education in private institutions when they have already paid taxes for public schools to educate their children. If parents were satisfied with their children's education in regular public schools, we doubt that these alternatives would be flourishing.

However, our concern is not with private schooling, it is with improving public schooling. Mainly we argue that public schools need to focus on the primary objective of educating students in a core curriculum, and that teachers need to instruct and principals need to manage for high effectiveness so that students are able to demonstrate high achievement. Many of our arguments and recommendations are directed toward this priority, and we hope they will enable parents, educators, and others to scrutinize the taken-for-granted ideas and practices in schools.

A number of our suggestions may surprise some readers, but we simply ask you to give them a fair hearing in the light of your own experience and judgment. The problems that exist in the current system of public education, and intelligent discussions about how we might address them, deserve the attention of us all, and we hope to make a contribution to these discussions.

Obviously, we think that much of our advice is common sense, and we believe most parents and citizens, as well as many teachers and administrators, will agree. Essentially, we argue that common sense should be a major benchmark in any consideration of school improvement. In this respect, we define common sense as sound judgment based on the wisdom of practical experience, the discernment arising from critical reflection, and the insight derived from specialized knowledge gained through systematic study and inquiry.

Our idea of common sense builds on the notion first articulated by the ancient Greek philosopher Aristotle because it values experiential knowledge, practical reason, and a test of utility, but it also incorporates expert knowledge and the evidence gained by systematic investigation, including educational research and scholarship. When common sense, as we define it, is represented in the judgment of educators and others, it should be given considerable weight in choosing a path to better schools.

Of course, our strong invocation of common sense has a certain risk. What counts as common sense to some people, to others merely reflects a view that is uninformed, misinformed, or perhaps even prejudiced. Precisely because of this risk, we incorporate systematic inquiry and study into our expanded notion of common sense as an antidote to ignorance, misunderstanding, and prejudice. That research and scholarship supports or does not support certain educational ideas and practices should be a qualification that all fair-minded people should be able to accept. But judging the import of research and scholarship for classrooms and schools also requires caution. Some research is better than other research because of the significance of the problem studied, the methods that are used, the reliability of the evidence, and the conclusions deduced from the findings.

In education, specifically, but also in the social sciences, generally, contested issues cannot be resolved by experiments as they can in many of the natural sciences. Of course, there is important systematic inquiry and research in education, but often the results of the research are not strong enough to identify exactly what teachers should or should not do in their specific classrooms.

Speaking technically, research in education on the variables that affect important outcomes of schooling, notably students' academic achievement, explains, at best, about 35 percent of the variation in those outcomes. Thus, about 65 percent of what matters in securing an effective educational experience is unexplained in the thousands of research studies that have been published over the last fifty years. The fact that research and scholarship in education is not definitive means that it is misleading for so-called experts to claim that "the research proves that teachers should do such-and-such." Thus, we argue that research suggests that doing one thing is generally more effective than doing something else, but no educational research proves what specific teachers should do with the unique group of students in their classrooms.

Practically, this means that teachers and administrators must rely more on their professional knowledge, judgment, and common sense than on scientific evidence in their classroom and school decision making. Given that teachers deal with large groups of students with a wide range of cognitive abilities, personal dispositions, and social experiences, it is essential for teachers and administrators to understand what research can realistically contribute to improving educational practices and students' learning. Frankly, the activities of teaching, learning, and school administration have considerable complexity and, therefore, limited predictability regarding the success of students.

Consequently, teachers, particularly those who have proven to be effective, must be allowed to rely on their professional judgment and common sense, including their understanding of what the research literature means for their particular situation, when deciding how best to deliver the required curriculum and evaluate their students' progress. Obviously, we cannot know about the specific circumstances that teachers and administrators need to consider; nevertheless, we think that there are certain things they should think about before they act. We base our analysis and advice on the research evidence that we think is most important and on argumentation that is most consistent with common sense as we have defined it. This means, of course, that our claims and advice may be contested. For this reason, we do not expect readers to agree with everything we recommend, and we certainly understand that you, the reader, will make up your own mind.

Essentially, this book reflects our perspective on a disagreement about the social mandate of schools and the institutional means by which that mandate is realized. In this disagreement, one orientation, represented by people such as Michael Apple (2006), William Ayers (2001), Paulo Freire (1970), Maxine Greene (1995), Alfie Kohn (1999), and Peter McLaren

(2002), encourages teachers to engage in social reform by being unapologetic advocates for the idea that teachers must help free students from the oppression of a narrow, inadequate perspective on the world. These "romantic progressives," as E. D. Hirsch Jr. (1996, 71–79) calls them, argue that social change begins in the classroom and teachers must lead the revolution to create a better society.

Heather Mac Donald (2000, 82–102), a fellow at the Manhattan Institute in New York, has summarized the romantic progressive orientation as the "anything but knowledge" school of educational thought. This is a harsh criticism, but it points discerningly to the failure of the progressives to respond seriously to the fundamental question that any educational advocate must answer, namely, "What knowledge is of most worth?" In their disparagement of traditional education, and as champions of developmental and naturalistic processes in learning and teaching, progressives often trivialize conventional knowledge and skills as less important than individual volition and self-esteem.

The progressive orientation is pitted against another orientation—traditional, and both conservative and liberal—represented by people such as William Bennett, Chester Finn Jr., and John Cribb Jr. (1999), Jay P. Greene (2005), E. D. Hirsch Jr. (1996), Diane Ravitch (2000), and in Canada, Mark Holmes (1998), who place much greater emphasis on ensuring students are knowledgeable and skillful in specific content areas and are educated to be successful in a complex modern society. We have the most regard for, and confidence in, the analyses and arguments of these writers because they wish to reform public education along lines that do not dismiss proven traditional practices, and they also recognize the importance of open discussion and debate on educational matters.

Nevertheless, advocates of romantic progressivism currently hold sway in the educational establishment and in many schools of education where teachers are trained (see Kramer 1991; Mac Donald 2000, 82–102). Even though there is some debate in schools of education, the assumptions and ideas of the progressives have considerable influence throughout North America. Among the advocates of this perspective, Alfie Kohn (1999) is perhaps the best known and the most popular. He is a persuasive spokesman, but we think that those of his persuasion are misguided or wrong. In short, we think that their analyses of the schooling mandate and some of the policies and practices they favor defy our notion of common sense and consequently are unwise.

Unfortunately, there is no guarantee that public schools will provide an education of high quality. In public schools, *caveat emptor* (buyer beware) must be observed by all who care about the education of children. There is no educational equivalent of the Better Business Bureau, and professional standards of practice invoked by the teaching profession, and other account-ability measures, where they exist, are less precise and less demanding than they are for other professions. In addition, schools of education are often reluctant to discuss, in a free and open manner, many of the controversial practices that they have been advising their graduating teachers to adopt. Not surprisingly, we think that schools of education are part of the problem because some of the practices they sponsor are inconsistent with our notion of common sense.

We think that public schools can become more effective for more students if they embrace a critical common sense that can subject the claims of the ro-mantic progressives to serious scrutiny. We hope that our book will empower parents, educators, and others who are themselves already fighting to improve schooling. Also, we hope that our ideas encourage teachers and school admin-istrators to question their own practices, and become more inclined to explain their educational practices to parents and other citizens.

In our view, results and outcomes relevant to the purposes of educa-tion should be the basis for the accountability of public schools (see Greene 2005). This accountability should not be anchored in excessive administrative oversight of the teaching process but in improved students' achievement. It should not be substituted for by the zeal of educational consultants or gurus earnest to have their innovations and prescriptions adopted by teachers, administrators, and school boards. If this means that some of our criticisms and recommendations are provocative to some teachers and administrators, school boards, professors of education, and state or provincial educational officials, then so be it. Trying to improve public schools should take prece-dence over gaining favor with those who are the educational establishment, an establishment that is not known for its robust debate of educational ideas and practices.

We engage in what may be called "the school wars" with skepticism about the reigning progressive ideology, and with specific attention to the most compelling contributions of common sense and educational research to improved educational practices. We believe that we should not discard educational practices merely because they are traditional. Rather, we should respect and sustain educational practices—both traditional and modern—that are proven to be successful. Furthermore, major educational innovations should be subjected to systematic evaluations so that we can scrutinize the claims of their sponsors. You may think that this means more research, testing, and assessment in schools. It does mean this, and we support such efforts wholeheartedly.

We also believe that the so-called progressives trivialize the school's role as an essential instrument of cultural preservation and transmission. They disagree that students need to encounter a socially mandated curriculum. In contrast, we argue that virtually all students who are capable must demonstrate the requisite knowledge and skills appropriate to a grade level before attempting the next one. Also, we argue that students are entitled to the educational rewards and benefits that flow from their ability, motivation, effort, and, of course, their achievements.

Therefore, we recommend, for example, that public schools must shift their focus to teaching and systematically evaluating students' achievement in core subjects, and to upholding discipline codes more rigorously, especially in secondary schools where the lessons of citizenship can begin to show mature expression. We believe that homework, when properly designed, is an appropriate way of reinforcing basic skills and developing students' responsibility and independence. Moreover, we see nothing wrong with saying that teachers must be knowledgeable about the subjects they teach and they must be able to deal critically with the promises of change advocates and other enthusiasts of the latest "research-based practices."

This book consists of fourteen chapters, which we organize into three parts. Part I includes six chapters and deals with fundamental aspects of educational arrangements and practices that have engendered enduring debate. Part II also includes six chapters and addresses specific practical issues that parents, teachers, and school administrators deal with on a continuing basis. Part III includes two chapters on aspects of the educational scene that distract people from the hard work of improving public schools.

Each of the fourteen chapters begins with a short prologue, a fictional story that illustrates the main issue being addressed, and concludes with a number of recommendations. While it is best to read the chapters in the order that they are presented, they can be read in any order because they are self-contained. Finally, we include an annotated bibliography at the end of each chapter as both references and suggested readings for those who want a deeper understanding of the issues.

BIBLIOGRAPHY

Apple, Michael W. 2006. *Educating the "right" way: Markets, standards, God, and inequality.* New York: Routledge.
Michael Apple identifies what he believes to be the major problems with the traditional approach to education.

Ayers, William. 2001. *To teach: The journey of a teacher.* New York: Teachers College Press.
William Ayers identifies the promotion of social justice as a key mandate for public schools and he is critical of reformers who place a stronger emphasis on the acquisition of knowledge and skills.

Bennett, William J., Chester E. Finn Jr., and John T. E. Cribb Jr. 1999. *The educated child: A parent's guide from preschool through eighth grade.* New York: The Free Press.
This book challenges the mediocrity found in many American public schools and identifies the core curriculum that all children should master at each grade.

Burke, Lindsey. 2009. *School choice in America 2009: What it means for children's futures.* Washington, DC: The Heritage Foundation.
This report shows that increasingly more parents are sending their children to both public and private schools of their choice.

Freire, Paulo. 1970. *Pedagogy of the oppressed.* New York: Continuum.
In this classic work, Paulo Freire critiques what he refers to as the "banking" theory of schooling and lays out his vision for using education to liberate oppressed people. Freire's work has been foundational for many of the romantic progressives.

Greene, Jay P. 2005. *Education myths: What special-interest groups want you to believe about our schools—and why it isn't so.* Lanham, MD: Rowman & Littlefield.
Greene debunks a number of education myths that dominate educational policy. He argues that these myths are, at best, only partial truths that, in fact, account for some of the resistance to educational reforms by teachers, school administrators, and citizens.

Greene, Maxine. 1995. *Releasing the imagination: Essays on education, the arts, and social change*. San Francisco, CA: Jossey-Bass.
A long-time advocate of the romantic progressive ideology in education outlines her vision for schools and the role of teachers.

Hirsch, E. D., Jr. 1996. *The schools we need and why we don't have them*. New York: Doubleday.
Well-known educational reformer E. D. Hirsch Jr. presents a case for requiring specific content to be taught and tested in public schools, and he counters the romantic progressives' ideas and practices that he sees as obstacles to obtaining more effective schools.

Holmes, Mark. 1998. *The reformation of Canada's schools: Breaking the barriers to parental choice*. Kingston, ON: McGill-Queen's University Press.
A retired school administrator and former professor of education at the Ontario Institute for Studies in Education, University of Toronto, argues vigorously against the dominant progressive mind-set and in favor of more traditional approaches to education. He also argues that parents need to have greater choices in the public schools their children attend.

Kohn, Alfie. 1999. *The schools our children deserve: Moving beyond traditional classrooms and "tougher" standards*. Boston, MA: Houghton Mifflin.
This book is an attack on traditional teaching methods and advocates for progressive methods.

Kramer, Rita. 1991. *Ed school follies: The miseducation of America's teachers*. New York: The Free Press.
Kramer, a well-known journalist, spent a year visiting schools of education across the United States. Her book provides considerable insight into the romantic progressive philosophy that informs many of the undergraduate and graduate degree programs in education.

Lips, Dan, Jennifer Marshall, and Lindsey Burke. 2008. *A parent's guide to education reform*. Washington, DC: The Heritage Foundation.
This monograph is written for parents and addresses problems in public schooling. The authors argue for greater accountability and more parental choice.

Mac Donald, Heather. 2000. *The burden of bad ideas: How modern intellectuals misshape our society*. Chicago: Ivan R. Dee.
In a chapter titled, "Why Johnny's Teacher Can't Teach," Heather Mac Donald takes direct aim at the romantic progressive ideology that has become dominant in many schools of education and public schools.

McLaren, Peter. 2002. *Critical pedagogy and predatory culture: Oppositional politics in a postmodern era.* New York: Routledge.
Peter McLaren is an education professor who sees education as primarily a quest for social justice rather than imparting knowledge and skills to the next generation of citizens.

Ravitch, Diane. 2000. *Left back: A century of failed school reforms.* New York: Simon & Schuster.
Education historian and former United States assistant secretary of education Diane Ravitch provides many examples of how the romantic progressive ideology has damaged public education over the last one hundred years.

SOME THINGS
ARE FUNDAMENTAL

1

Subject Matter Matters

PROLOGUE

"What a month it has been," thought Brian Taylor to himself as he wrapped up his first month of full-time university studies. His course load wasn't supposed to be anything out of the ordinary. He was taking introductory courses in calculus, American history, English literature, biology, and psychology. Since Brian had not decided on a definite career path, he felt it was important to take a variety of courses in his first year so that he could keep his options open.

As Brian replayed the events of the month in his mind, there was little doubt that high school had not prepared him for what he was experiencing in university. On his first day of classes, he had received the shock of his life when Professor Daniel Stevenson informed his 150 American history students that their first test would be in three weeks and would cover everything from the earliest American settlements until the inauguration of President George Washington in 1789. "It took us almost half the semester in my high school course to study the American Revolution and now I'm expected to relearn all that stuff in just three weeks!" exclaimed Brian to himself. "Looks like the expectations here are a little higher than what I was used to in high school."

His calculus class was not going any better. While Brian had received good marks in the pre-calculus course in high school, he was struggling to understand the material in his university course. "I wish that we had spent less time inventing our own ways to understand math in high school and more time actually learning how to solve real problems," murmured Brian in quiet frustration.

Needless to say, Brian was also taken aback by the amount of work required in his English literature class. "I can't believe that they expect me to read the entire two thousand pages of the *Norton Anthology of English Literature* in just one course. We studied only a few short novels in Grade 12 English and the teacher even read most of them to us during class. And how in the world can I write four twelve-page essays in this course when I wrote only two five-page essays in my last year of high school? Maybe doing the puppet show for the kindergarten students instead of writing a research essay wasn't such a bright idea after all," thought Brian.

After spending a little more time pondering his predicament, Brian figured that it was time to get to work. He had tests to write in his biology and psychology courses tomorrow, and he knew that he needed to do a lot more studying. Since Brian had been unfamiliar with virtually all of the topics in these courses when the year began, he had spent a lot of time reviewing his notes and reading the textbooks. He was worried that all this work still wouldn't be enough.

"Why didn't my teachers prepare me better for some of this in high school?" wondered Brian. "After twelve years of schooling, I feel like I hardly learned anything at all and I am just beginning to learn how to study properly."

INTRODUCTION

Brian is finding out the hard way just how little his public school education has prepared him for the rigors of postsecondary education in terms of content and expectations. While Brian Taylor may be fictional, his experience certainly is not. It is repeated across Canada and the United States every year as many first-year students discover how unprepared they are for their college and university courses. In fact, colleges and universities have even gone so far as to institute special remedial mathematics and writing courses in an attempt to make up for the serious academic deficiencies in many of their incoming students. By not providing sufficient academic content and rigor, public schools do a disservice to the students and to society when they graduate students who are inadequately prepared for postsecondary education or for employment.

However, the problems experienced by postsecondary students are merely a symptom of a much larger problem. Too many students are being short-changed when schools embrace educational approaches that undermine the importance of content mastery and specific performance standards. Instead of ensuring that students graduate with the knowledge and skills they need, many public schools focus on enhancing their students' self-esteem, or they let teachers become distracted by unproven instructional and evaluation practices that dilute the pursuit of excellence, trivialize the learning of content, and ignore the necessity for the sustained development of traditional academic skills.

We cannot continue on this disturbing path without serious consequences. Society needs well-educated citizens, and students need to be well-educated to make their way in a modern, economically competitive society. Unfortunately, public schools are failing in this important task.

WHAT IS THE PURPOSE OF SCHOOLING?

For the average person, this question is really not that difficult to answer. Central to what most people expect of schools is that they are institutions where students gain the requisite knowledge, skills, and values to function effectively in contemporary society, both as workers and citizens. Children come to school to be taught by teachers because they do not yet have the knowledge, skills, and values that they are going to need in their lives. This is the most basic idea of education as understood by most parents and, not surprisingly, by most university and college educators. Most people think it is common sense.

Rightly understood, conventional public expectations of schools highlight a persuasive logic as old as Aristotle. This Greek philosopher of 2,500 years ago held that the good of human beings lies in the exercise of their intelligence or reason in the pursuit of excellence, virtue, and the good life in order to be happy and to become contributing members of society. Because there is a link between the individual and society, both individually oriented and socially oriented expectations have legitimacy in schools.

For example, because the individually oriented expectation of having a good job is satisfying for the individual and is advantageous for the economic order of society, schools are expected to help prepare young people in important ways for successful employment. And because the socially oriented expectation of effective citizenship contributes to individuals' satisfying political participation and the good of society, the preparation of young people for effective citizenship is also a defensible task for schools. Much the same could be said for other perceived aims of schooling. That is, the basic task of schooling is to provide for both the well-being of the individuals and social harmony, both anticipated by the cultivation of reasonably independent learners who can think for themselves.

If the use of one's intelligence and talents in a balanced pursuit of the good life is the overarching aim of schooling, then what educational program for children and youth would be most consistent with this aim? Obviously, the school curriculum and related school experiences deserve our attention, as does the pedagogy of teachers—how teachers teach and how they are taught in schools of education. Certainly conventional public expectations of schooling suggest that the curriculum and related school experiences should provide the means and the opportunity for students' personal growth and the cultivation of their individual talents while addressing socially valued knowledge and skills.

While this basic task may seem merely a matter of common sense, it is not especially evident in the mission statements of many North American public school boards. Here we often find references to nebulous notions of "community building," "learning communities," or "the unique needs of each child" but rarely do we see references to the promotion of standards of excellence or the preparation of knowledgeable and skillful graduates.

This real example is quite typical: "[Our school jurisdiction] is a community of learners, every one of whom shares responsibility to assist children in acquiring an education which will enable them to lead fulfilling lives within the world as moral people and contributing members of society." At this level of generality, much of this statement is easy to agree with; however, it is fair, even necessary, for parents, teachers, school board members, and others to ask exactly how the educational program will promote personal fulfillment, moral discernment, intelligent citizenship, and productive, satisfying lives for those who graduate from the schools.

Is schooling fundamentally about "building a community of learners?" Even if we accept that it is, the accomplishment of this social objective, worthy as it may be, is likely impossible if students don't come to possess the essential knowledge, skills, and values needed to function in society with competence and comfort. Is there not a fundamental knowledge base, a compendium of concepts and skills that needs to be grasped by members of society for the advantage of individuals and for the benefit of all? And is not the school the key institution where we expect students to acquire the strong foundation for learning it?

As Robin Barrow (1981, 111) has wisely observed: "At a basic level, reading, writing and numeracy are obviously vital skills both for our way of life and as a means to education. These must not be left to chance." Equally, we expect school graduates to be familiar with the important ideas and achievements in the sciences, literature, and the arts, and to have a basic understanding of at least their own nation's history, society, and government.

In the renowned *The Padeia Proposal*, Mortimer Adler (1982) and his associates identified the three major areas of language, literature, and fine arts; mathematics and natural sciences; and history, geography, and social studies as crucial to a twelve-year program of schooling. For them, these three main areas of knowledge "comprise the most fundamental branches of learning [and] provide the learner with indispensable knowledge about nature and culture, the world in which we live, our social institutions, and ourselves" (Adler 1982, 23–24).

Former University of Virginia professor E. D. Hirsch Jr. (2006) calls this knowledge base cultural literacy. We share Hirsch's belief that it is possible to identify what students need to know and understand, and that there are ways of accurately testing whether or not schools are attending to this knowledge base adequately. Unfortunately, this will not happen if schools allow their emphasis on community building and self-esteem to lead them to neglect a curriculum that focuses on specific content and skills.

Perhaps an analogy will be helpful in underscoring this point. Every year, thousands of teenagers across North America enroll in driver education classes and they do so for a very specific reason. They want to be able to pass the driving test and receive a driver's license so they can legally drive a car or motorbike. What would we think if driver education instructors were to announce that they didn't think it was necessary to require specific knowledge in their courses about what driving necessarily involves, including the everyday skills of steering, signaling, and parking, some basic knowledge of power and engine mechanics, car maintenance, and road safety?

Of course, every driver is unique; all of them have their own ways of driving; but some ways are obviously better than others. What if, in place of specific driving standards, driving instructors proposed that their primary focus was on valuing the uniqueness of all members of their community? Would people actually enroll their children in driver education schools that had "Uniqueness Begins Here" as their mission statement?

While the answers to these questions are, we hope, self-evident, the sad reality is that too many educators favor this murky path for schools. If we expect driver education instructors to provide specific knowledge and skills to produce proficient drivers, why would we expect less from public school teachers in other subject areas? We assert that it is not unreasonable to lay out specific expectations for what children should know and be able to do skillfully by the end of each grade, and no one should graduate from high school without possessing the basic knowledge and skills that are the necessary foundation for successful livelihood and effective citizenship.

CONTENT MATTERS

While we will not review all the theories about how children learn, we wish to comment on a particular educational philosophy, constructivism, that has had a major impact on teaching methodologies in North American schools. Constructivism asserts that people learn by constructing meaning based on their existing knowledge. In other words, people learn best when they are able to relate new information to something with which they are already familiar. As a result, there is little point in explaining a new concept to someone without a point of reference that is understood. So, not surprisingly, someone who has lived his whole life in a tropical climate will have much more difficulty understanding what snow is than someone who grew up in a place where snow is common during winter.

At this point, most readers are probably thinking that constructivism, when described in this way, makes a lot of sense. And they would be right. We do, in fact, learn best when we are able to relate new information to something we already know. But, this is not a new idea. Aristotle, the Greek philosopher we mentioned earlier, knew this. Today, many people would probably think that this is just common sense. Throwing random facts at students without providing a context that is understandable to them is indeed a very poor way to teach. One could argue that virtually every piece of knowledge is constructed by the recipient in one form or another. So why then have we identified constructivism as a problematic philosophy?

The answer is very simple. Unfortunately, a common conclusion based on the constructivist perspective is that there are no absolutes; in other words, no construction or understanding is better than any other. When this assumption is accepted, it is tempting to conclude that conventional content and facts don't really matter much. Why have students learn typical interpretations and facts about major historical events when we can have them construct their own "understanding" about why things are the way they are? In addition, if no piece of prose has any absolute meaning, then English teachers are free to encourage their students to make whatever book or prose they read mean whatever they want, regardless of the author's intent.

When this happens, classrooms cease to be places of learning and become social laboratories; places where teachers experiment with the minds of students. While we accept that knowledge is, to a certain degree, socially constructed, we assert that there are relatively objective standards for the worth of what can be constructed. For example, gravity will continue to be a force that pulls us down to the earth regardless of how we choose to construct our understanding of it.

When taken to extremes, constructivism is used to justify some rather dubious teaching practices. In North American schools, there is a strong emphasis on practices such as project-based learning, discovery learning, inquiry learning, hands-on learning, and cooperative learning. At the same time, there is a push to reduce the amount of time students spend on teacher-directed instruction, the memorization of facts, and formal testing.

While it is easy to agree with one aspect of the constructivist claim, namely that learning must be an active process, Robert Marzano (2003, 108), for example, warns that "this principle is frequently over-generalized to mean that teachers should rarely (if ever) teach content to students." He suggests that constructivist models of instruction, naively or mistakenly applied, undermine proven teaching practices and unwisely replace them with practices that discourage the mastery of specific and necessary content that secures the correct understanding of the subject area.

To illustrate this danger, let's take a look at some specific subjects. Most of us remember mathematics as a subject where following correct procedure usually led to the correct answer. To solve a mathematics problem, one needed first to be clear what the problem was, what the correct steps were, to follow them, and perform the calculations properly. Lots of math drill was necessary because it took time and practice to learn the basic procedures. To master the procedures so they can be performed efficiently, students also had to memorize the multiplication table and other important pieces of information.

Teachers spent a lot of time explaining the protocols and techniques of attacking problems and guiding students through several examples. Students were then expected to complete assignments consisting of a series of similar problems that became progressively more difficult. Fortunately, if you paid attention in class, and if you applied the procedures correctly, you were likely to complete the assignments successfully. The questions assigned would be corrected the next day and, assuming most of the students performed satisfactorily, the teacher would move on to the next topic and repeat a similar procedure.

According to progressive educators, the problem with this model is that it relies too heavily on rote memorization. Today, teachers are told that rote exercises, such as memorizing multiplication tables, need to be replaced by open-ended word problems that encourage students to come up with a variety of possible answers. In keeping with this philosophy, the National Council of Teachers of Mathematics has published standards that de-emphasize the learning of factual content and procedures to the level where they are "automatic" and show "controlled processing." Instead, the Council's document notes that "most of the arithmetic and algebraic procedures long viewed as the heart of the school mathematics curriculum can now be performed with handheld calculators. Thus, more attention can be given to understanding the number concepts and the modeling procedures used in problem solving" (National Council of Teachers of Mathematics 2000, 20).

However, one of the results of students being encouraged to discover their own way to solve "real-life" mathematical problems is that the most efficient problem-solving techniques are not adequately modeled or taught and effective practice to achieve "automaticity and controlled processing" is neglected. A related sad outcome of this form of teaching is that we are ending up with a generation of citizens who are too dependent on calculators and computers for solving even the simplest of mathematical calculations.

The same dilution of the curriculum can be seen in subjects such as social studies and science. Since constructivism, so understood, dictates that students create their own understanding of the world, why would we expect students to know, even memorize, certain dates in history courses and know their significance, or why would a teacher directly teach them about scientific accomplishments? As a result, students spend a lot of time on self-discovery projects that, while effective at responding to individual interests, may not be sufficient to teach them the essential ideas and facts in the important fields of history and science. Having students try to discover the principles underlying the periodic table in chemistry seems foolish when we know that these principles have taken scientists years to figure out.

English Language Arts (or French Language Arts, in certain Canadian schools) is the subject that has seen perhaps the largest transformation over the last few decades. It has gone from a subject rich in content to a hodge-podge of incoherent exercises where students learn practically nothing of substance or specific communication skills. Ironically, English is the subject that usually will have the most learning outcomes listed and the longest and most detailed curriculum guides. Sadly, one cannot easily find specific standards in many of these guides. With outcomes such as "students will learn how to celebrate their community," it is not surprising that virtually any classroom activity can be justified as the content of English and that some teachers will be puzzled about their instructional mandate.

Again, we are increasingly faced with the regrettable outcome that some students can barely write a coherent paragraph when they graduate from high school. Is this because important skills such as using proper spelling and grammar are barely mentioned in many English curriculum guides or gain little attention in many English classrooms? We think that the poor reading and writing skills of a large number of high school graduates is a travesty. Surely our students can do better, and they deserve better.

Thus, we believe that the teaching of specific content in schools does matter and that it is possible to specify with adequate precision what students should know by the time they finish high school. Doing so will require replacing the questionable practices that have too much currency in many schools with clear and specific achievement standards based on an explicit curriculum that aims at mature cultural literacy. While this is a major undertaking, we believe that concrete measures can be taken to reverse the current trend.

RECOMMENDATIONS

Too often parents have suffered in silence while they have watched their children struggle, and they have seen school work that does not clearly identify the requirements of the curriculum and the children's mastery of it. Rather than directly challenging the educational system, an increasing number of parents have chosen to home-school their children, enroll them in private schools, or supplement their education with evening or summer sessions at one of the many Sylvan or Kumon Learning Centers across North America.

But we think it is unfortunate that so many parents cannot count on the public school system to teach their children what they need to know. All citizens support public schools through their taxes, and parents should be able to have the educational needs of their children met in the system they help fund. Certainly, parents should not pay private agencies to teach their children the basic skills and knowledge that are the responsibilities of the public school system.

For this reason, parents need to bring their concerns directly to their school board members, school administrators, and the teachers of their children. In jurisdictions where the state and provincial governments set the curriculum, elected representatives who are responsible for education should be approached to explain and justify the policies they have enacted. Parents should make it clear that they are not satisfied with a school curriculum that contains fuzzy curricular outcomes, lacks specific content and achievement standards, and trivializes systematic achievement tests. School boards need to be encouraged, even pressured, to address such dissatisfaction and the concerns that parents have for a stronger emphasis on the core subjects, and school boards should require specific achievement standards before allowing students to be promoted.

The Core Knowledge Foundation, an independent organization founded by E. D. Hirsch Jr. in 1986, has published detailed lists of specific content standards for each grade level from K–8. We encourage interested parents and educators to check out the foundation's website at coreknowledge.org to find ways to promote cultural literacy. A large number of public and private schools (over 750 at the time of this writing) in North America have registered to become official core knowledge schools.

Parents and teachers should consider what specific steps they can take to encourage their school board members and principals to make their schools into core knowledge institutions or to formally adopt comparable subject matter goals and achievement standards. In short, parents and educators need to work together to make sure children get the education they deserve. School officials need to hear clearly from parents and educators that yes, subject matter matters in schools.

BIBLIOGRAPHY

Adler, Mortimer J. 1982. *The Paideia proposal: An educational manifesto.* New York: Macmillan.
This book identifies the three major areas of language, literature, and fine arts; mathematics and natural sciences; and history, geography, and social studies as crucial to a twelve-year program of schooling.

Barrow, Robin. 1981. *The philosophy of schooling.* New York: John Wiley and Sons.
This book emphasizes that the central concern of schooling is the development of a wide cognitive perspective without sacrificing a concern for socialization, individual well-being, and the preparation of students for life.

Bennett, William J., Chester E. Finn Jr., and John T. E. Cribb Jr. 1999. *The educated child: A parent's guide from preschool through eighth grade.* New York: The Free Press.
This is an important book that critically examines the general direction of modern schools, and recommends that parents take action to ensure their children understand certain things at specific grade levels. The senior author, William Bennett, was secretary of education under President Ronald Reagan.

Hirsch, E. D., Jr. 1996. *The schools we need and why we don't have them.* New York: Doubleday.
In this book, well-known educational reformer E. D. Hirsch Jr. presents a strong case for requiring specific content to be taught and tested in schools. He also criticizes some of the ideas and practices in public schools that he thinks frustrate the achievement of this objective.

Hirsch, E. D., Jr. 2006. *The knowledge deficit: Closing the shocking education gap for American children.* Boston, MA: Houghton Mifflin.
This book argues that poor curriculum content is the primary cause of the poor reading comprehension skills of American students.

Marzano, Robert J. 2003. *What works in schools: Translating research into action.* Alexandria, VA: Association for Supervision and Curriculum Development.
The author argues that if we act on the results of the most reputable educational research we can achieve unprecedented effectiveness in public education.

National Council of Teachers of Mathematics. 2000. *Principles and standards for
school mathematics.* Reston, VA: Author.
This document sets out the principles and standards that the Council believes
should guide the teaching of mathematics in the K–12 schools at the beginning of
the twenty-first century.

2

Tests Are Good for Students

PROLOGUE

Melanie Davis couldn't wait for this day to be over. As a Grade 8 homeroom teacher for the last twenty-nine years at Elmwood Middle School, she'd had many busy days. Between an active group of twenty-eight students, a busy extracurricular schedule, and assignments to mark, most days provided her with plenty of challenges.

Those challenges were nothing compared to her frustrating in-service days, of which today was one. Her school district was putting on a session entitled "Implementing Authentic Assessment in the Classroom" that was going to take the whole day. The school district's newly hired assessment consultant, Dr. Randy Erickson, was explaining why the superintendent was replacing end-of-year examinations with process-based checklists that would be filled out by teachers throughout the year. In addition, Dr. Erickson strongly urged teachers to minimize their use of unit tests because, in his words, they harmed the learning process by making students focus on the test rather than on the actual learning.

This was too much for Melanie. "Excuse me, Dr. Erickson," interrupted Melanie, "but I don't understand how properly designed tests are harmful to students. In my classroom, I find that regular unit tests and final examinations, too, are an excellent way to find out what students have learned. When I know my students' strengths and weaknesses, I can structure my lessons to fill in the gaps that have been identified by those tests. Of course, tests are not perfect, but how can they be harmful to students? I don't understand."

Dr. Erickson hardly missed a beat. "Thanks for your question, Melanie. I respect teachers with your experience, but while many people believe that exams are useful, it is important to note that some recent research shows that high-stakes testing is harmful to the self-esteem of students. Also, the results of these tests reflect their ability to take tests rather than assessing what they have actually learned. We still will assess our students' learning, but we will do it differently. In fact, the new process-based checklists will actually convey more information about the students' learning than tests that capture only a snapshot of their achievement on a particular day," concluded Dr. Erickson.

"That may be so," replied Melanie, "but this new system sounds a lot more complicated than using tests and exams. I just don't have time to gather and organize all that data. And, how are we supposed to convey all of the information to parents so they have an accurate and complete picture of the achievement of their children?"

Dr. Erickson frowned and seemed annoyed. "Part of our responsibility as professionals is to ensure that our practices conform to what the research is demonstrating. High-stakes tests are an impediment to authentic learning, and this is something that we need to help parents understand. The district will be sending letters home to inform parents about the new assessment policy, but it is up to us, as professionals, to help parents understand why these changes are necessary."

Seeing little point in continuing with questions, Melanie nodded her head and fell silent. For the rest of the day, she dutifully listened to Dr. Erickson as he continued to criticize formal tests as an outdated form of student assessment. She was annoyed with the way she was being treated, at the arrogance of Dr. Erickson, and his ignoring of the arguments for formal testing.

At the end of the day, Melanie was still frustrated, and as she drove home thoughts kept going through her mind about what she had heard. "I don't understand what is wrong with giving students a formal test based on the curriculum to find out what they know. Both our students and their parents expect it, and it also helps me determine whether I have done a good job teaching the curriculum. I know that students often get nervous before writing a test, but I've always found that those who take the time to study are the ones who perform well. Isn't that how it's supposed to be?"

INTRODUCTION

Unfortunately, Melanie's situation is not uncommon for many teachers. Formal tests are regularly maligned by many education experts as an outdated form of assessment that must be replaced by more "authentic" assessments; by checklists, portfolios, group projects, and self-assessments, for example. Teachers and parents who are skeptical of, or actively resist, these modern methods of assessing students are labeled as old-school traditionalists who need to change with the times.

Similarly, bringing up the topic of standardized examinations with officials in teachers' unions or with many education professors usually results in teachers or parents being informed that these tests are among the worst things that can be foisted on children. These critics claim that subjecting students to the rigors of standardized examinations will kill their love of learning and turn them into mindless individuals who simply regurgitate questionable material on demand. Are such beliefs correct? We think not. In fact, well-designed tests are among the best tools that have been developed to ensure that students learn the mandated curriculum.

WHAT ARE TESTS AND WHY ARE THEY USED?

What is a test? The *Merriam-Webster* dictionary defines tests as "a series of questions or exercises for measuring the skill, knowledge, intelligence, capacities, or aptitudes of an individual or group." Most tests are a formal series of questions that students are required to answer without assistance from other people and without relying on other material.

Tests aren't limited to courses in schools and they are frequently used in everyday life. For example, cashiers who work for large grocery stores are expected to know the product codes for all the fruits and vegetables. In many cases, they are required to pass a formal test to work as a cashier. People who want a driver's license are required to pass both a written test and a driving test before they are allowed to drive a car by themselves. And, if you are an immigrant seeking to become a citizen, you will find yourself studying for a citizenship test that you need to pass before being granted citizenship.

Because of the amount that students are expected to learn and because teaching is structured so that subsequent learning benefits from prior teaching and understanding, it is only reasonable to expect that there must be a systematic and fair way of assessing whether or not students are learning the material they have been taught. Such testing should occur both as their knowledge and skills are developing (what educators call formative evaluation) and when the knowledge and skills become, given practice and correction, secure and confident, shown by the students' accurate demonstration or application of what has been learned (called summative evaluation).

If a class of Grade 5 students has spent several weeks learning how to perform long division using an algorithm, does it not make sense for them to show that they can actually do long division and apply it to real life situations like calculating the cost of items of food in a grocery store before moving on to other topics in mathematics? If a teacher has spent a couple of weeks teaching the history of the nation, the students should be able to identify the key people, events, and dates, and a formal unit test is certainly one way to have them do that.

Checklists, self-assessments, and group projects have their place as forms of continuous, or formative, evaluation of knowledge and skills, partly because they help teachers plan and adapt their teaching to the needs of their students. But, while it is true that teachers are constantly assessing their students on an informal basis, these techniques alone are insufficient for the purposes of instruction in schools. A test administered after a topic has been taught with adequate time for students to practice the skills they have learned is the most accurate, efficient, and fair method of determining whether the students have actually learned what they are supposed to have learned and possess a degree of independence in using or applying the knowledge and/or skills accurately.

This type of testing is essential, especially if a mandated curriculum is to be meaningful and if the public's confidence in public schools is to be sustained. When it is important to know the degree of success of the student for subsequent, advanced learning, such as entry to a postsecondary program, then testing serves an important qualifying or credentialing purpose. Schools must be able to serve several purposes for testing and they cannot ignore the necessity to do it competently and fairly.

Choosing to forgo summative tests in schools would be similar to providing student drivers with several weeks of driving practice but not requiring them to actually drive a car during a driver's test because they would have already demonstrated their ability to drive during the course they have been taking. The absurdity of this suggestion should make it clear why it makes no sense to abandon summative tests, because they are one of the best tools for helping students demonstrate their learning and for teachers to monitor the success of their teaching. But, just as it is important to distinguish between formative and summative assessment, it is also important to distinguish between standardized and unstandardized tests.

WHAT ABOUT STANDARDIZED TESTS?

Standardized tests are simply large-scale tests that are administered to large numbers of students, in a formal way, at a particular time, for a particular recognized purpose. They are also marked using specific protocols. A test is said to be standardized for a particular group of students if the format, administration, and marking are consistent, regardless of the classroom or school that the students are attending. One of the best known standardized tests in North America is the SAT Reasoning Test, which has also been called the Scholastic Aptitude Test and the Scholastic Assessment Test, which consists of a series of questions primarily about language and mathematics. SAT scores are used in conjunction with high school grades and other information to help admission officers at universities and colleges in the United States determine the suitability of students for the rigors of postsecondary education.

Why would postsecondary institutions require that their potential students take the SAT? Why not simply rely on high school grades when determining their admissions? You've probably already guessed the answer because it is common sense. Academic standards can vary considerably from school to school, and even from teacher to teacher within a school. Some teachers with high expectations may have very few students earning an A while others with lower expectations may have virtually all students earning an A.

If you were a university admissions officer, would you not want a more objective assessment to ensure that the best students are admitted? Furthermore, the SAT Reasoning Test provides a more objective assessment of the students' academic ability. The SAT Reasoning Test is certainly not a perfect assessment tool, but it is often better than the grades given by teachers.

The same argument can be made for public schools. It makes sense to have a balance between teacher-created assessments, which often vary from teacher to teacher, and standardized assessments, which do not vary from class to class or from school to school. Teachers are able to take local conditions into account when making their own tests, while standardized tests ensure that the knowledge and skills embedded in an established curriculum are being taught and learned. Fortunately, most Canadian provinces and most states in the United States use at least a few standardized tests. Nevertheless, many teachers' unions and professors of education disparage standardized tests as being unfair and not authentic. Let's look at some of their arguments to see whether they constitute a strong case for getting rid of this form of assessment.

ARE ARGUMENTS AGAINST STANDARDIZED TESTS PERSUASIVE?

There are five common arguments made against the use of standardized tests in public schools, namely that these tests are biased against minority students, they are not authentic, they force teachers to teach to the test, they undermine the professional autonomy of teachers, and they cause stress to students. We examine these arguments in turn.

1. Standardized Tests Are Unfairly Biased against Minority Students

A number of educators and union leaders say that it is unfair to require all students to take the same tests because students who are more familiar with the majority culture will have an inherent advantage over those who are unfamiliar with this culture. For example, recent immigrants from Caribbean countries would likely have more difficulty interpreting questions involving the words "winter," "snow," and "Christmas tree," while students who have lived in Canada or the northern part of the United States would have no difficulty understanding these words. As we all know, there are many other examples of popular phrases and sayings that are second nature to some students, but could be alien to students who have been brought up in other cultures.

There are two main problems with this objection. First, if it is possible to identify examples of bias on standardized tests, it is also possible to correct those biases. Rather than simply throwing out the entire test because of a few examples of bias, why not make the necessary adjustments to ensure that the tests are fairer and more objective? One cannot, on one hand, claim that standardized tests are biased against minority groups, but, on the other hand, not correct the biases by redesigning the tests or adjusting the scoring. In fact, the testing experts who design standardized tests like the SAT work diligently to reduce these biases, and generally they have been very successful.

The second major problem with this objection is that it seems to question the ability of public school teachers to help all students learn the material they need to know. Teachers regularly provide special assistance to students who are disadvantaged because of their linguistic or cultural experiences, and it is reasonable to think that this assistance would be provided when disadvantaged students are preparing to write standardized tests. The whole point of having a common curriculum is to provide all students with a common set of skills and knowledge so that they can function effectively in society. Since standardized tests are designed to assess these important skills and knowledge, it is possible for teachers to help bring most, if not all, students up to the minimum level that is required to pass the tests.

Of course, we recognize that there are some exceptions to this general rule. Students with severe cognitive disabilities or those with little understanding of English (or French in some Canadian schools) should logically be exempt from taking standardized tests. Nevertheless, this does not change the fact that the large majority of students should have little difficulty in taking and passing standardized tests on the curriculum they are required to learn. Of course, they will need to prepare, practice, and study to pass the test, but surely this is a normal expectation for students.

2. Standardized Tests Are Not an Authentic Form of Assessment

To properly address this objection, it is important to define what is meant by authentic assessment. Grant Wiggins (1990), a leading advocate of authentic assessment, defines it as an assessment of students' performances on worthy intellectual tasks. Believing that standardized tests are artificial constructs that only measure a very narrow range of simple skills, Wiggins maintains that they lack authenticity. Instead, he argues that students should be engaged in deep, meaningful activities that make use of their constructed understanding of the world around them.

In reality, it is Wiggins's argument that lacks authenticity. Of course, it makes sense for students to perform tasks that are related to the real world, and for teachers to help students acquire a deep, not superficial, understanding of the world. However, agreeing with Wiggins about the importance of meaningful understanding does not mean that standardized tests cannot measure, to a considerable degree, the students' understanding of important "real world" things.

This argument provides no reason to conclude that well-designed standardized tests cannot be part of an effective assessment program. Multiple-choice items and short-answer questions are, in fact, excellent ways of finding out whether students have mastered key concepts. Getting students to perform basic mathematical tasks, know the significance of key historical events, identify important scientific achievements, and use proper grammar are all examples of relevant foundational skills that can be evaluated through well-designed standardized tests.

No one is arguing that standardized tests should be used instead of other formal and informal types of assessment. Rather, standardized tests must be one of several types of instruments that good teachers use to determine if their students are learning what they are teaching. To eliminate any of the normal testing instruments, specifically standardized tests, would result in a grave disservice to students and parents; indeed, it could be considered a form of professional malpractice. Imagine what patients would think of an optometrist who refused to use the standardized instruments and procedures to assess their eyes.

3. Standardized Tests Cause Teachers to Teach to the Test

All tests, whether standardized or teacher-created, formative or summative, are expected to mirror the curriculum. Thus, teaching to the test means that teachers are, in fact, teaching to the curriculum, which is exactly what they should be doing. Do we accuse driving instructors of blindly teaching to the test when they make their students practice parallel parking? Of course not. Parallel parking is an important part of the test because it is an integral part of driving competently.

Similarly, most standardized tests that are used in schools cover important aspects of the curriculum that teachers are expected to teach and students are expected to learn. These tests are called criterion-referenced because they are based on the curriculum; that is, these tests are based on the mandated knowledge and skills that is the criterion for the test.

Simply put, these standardized tests assess whether the teachers have taught the curriculum and whether the students have learned it. To do otherwise is unfair to the students because the mandated curriculum is what students can reasonably be held accountable for in their achievement. So, we hope that teachers are teaching to the test. If they aren't, then they probably aren't following the mandated curriculum. If this is the case, parents and school administrators should be concerned and together they should help correct this problem.

4. Standardized Tests Undermine the Professional Autonomy of Teachers

This is another specious point. Do standardized eye examinations undermine the professional autonomy of optometrists? Does requiring police officers to correctly use a standardized breathalyzer when determining a suspect's intoxication level bring into question the professional autonomy of police officers? Of course not.

In virtually every profession, standardized instruments and procedures are mandated, and professionals are expected to correctly use those instruments. If they don't, they can face malpractice suits. Thus, rather than undermining the professional autonomy of teachers, standardized tests and procedures actually enhance their autonomy. They are objective instruments that teachers can use to demonstrate that they are fulfilling their professional responsibilities; specifically, teachers are teaching the mandated curriculum and the students are learning it.

We emphasize that we are not advocating that standardized tests are the only form of assessment to be used by teachers. Obviously, teachers should use informal observations, projects, portfolios, and tests to help them understand how well their students are learning. Just as it would be unwise to use only teacher-made tests, it would be equally unwise to use only standardized assessments.

5. Standardized Tests Cause Students to Suffer Significant Stress That Harms Their Self-Esteem

This argument is only mentioned because it has actually been presented as a serious argument by some educators. These educators ignore the fact that not all stress is harmful. Most of us know that a certain amount of stress is required to get things done, and we need to distinguish between the kinds and levels of stress. In most occupations, employees are subjected to at least moderate levels of stress and this can serve as a powerful motivator to get a job done and to do it well. Employees who never face any stress are most likely to become bored, listless, and careless.

Students, particularly young students, are not workers, of course, but they can also become bored if what they are required to learn is not sufficiently challenging, which means that learning itself causes some stress. There is nothing wrong with students feeling some moderate levels of anxiety prior to taking a test. A test provides a challenge, and challenges can cause stress. For virtually all students, a moderate level of anxiety can be a powerful motivator for careful preparation, for reviewing the material, and for practicing the skills. It also helps them focus their attention on the material while they are writing the formal test. In contrast, if students are never challenged to achieve their best, they are unlikely to put the effort that is required into review, practice, and study. And if they don't do these things, students are not likely to understand the subject matter as well as they should.

It is obvious that competitions in sports and music, which are a type of standardized assessment, are important for athletes and musicians even when they are young. Children, in fact, improve their performances because they put considerable effort into practicing before competing. During competitions, children recognize how successful they are, and their parents recognize how well they have done. Both children and parents also see what needs work before the next competition.

Similarly, good teachers help their students practice academic skills so they become competent. Good teachers also use formal assessments to ensure that their students have learned the curriculum and can demonstrate their understanding. It is very important for teachers to make sure that their students are prepared for formal tests by teaching them what they need to know.

So, are these arguments against formal tests, particularly standardized tests, persuasive? We think not. The abandonment of standardized testing of students' achievement is unwise because it is a necessary part of an effective educational program and a reputable program of evaluation and assessment. And assessment is a fundamental part of teaching in all subjects and grade levels. We say, let teachers use many ways to assess their students' learning as long as their assessments accurately reflect the curriculum and the achievement of their students.

RECOMMENDATIONS

Obviously, we believe that tests, both teacher-created and standardized, ought to be an integral part of the learning process in schools. While we recognize that no form of evaluation or assessment is perfect, we think there are good reasons for schools to have a formal and regular testing regime at all grade levels. This regime should include standardized tests, especially at the middle and high school levels where such tests have increased validity and reliability.

When students do not understand the curriculum, teachers must know this as soon as possible so they can adjust their teaching accordingly. In addition, parents have a right to know how their children are doing, and formal tests are one of the best ways of evaluating their performance. Why shouldn't teachers and schools use standardized instruments to serve their students' and their parents' interests more effectively? Obviously, we think they should, either as an integral part of state and provincial testing programs on the mandated curriculum, or as an aspect of a similar testing program sponsored by the local school jurisdiction.

Consequently, we recommend that parents ask for the results of their children's performance on standardized tests as well as their achievement results on teacher-made tests and projects because formative and summative evaluation, though complementary, have somewhat different purposes, as we have noted earlier. Moreover, we believe that all prospective teachers must receive thorough training in how to properly design and use a wide repertoire of tests and other assessment techniques.

There is no case for limiting this repertoire to so-called authentic assessment as some education professors and in-service gurus recommend. Rather, prospective teachers need to be taught how to construct good assessment instruments and how to use a variety of instruments that have been constructed by experts. Properly constructed tests, both teacher-made and standardized, are important tools that good teachers should use to ensure that their students are learning the curriculum. Tests are, in fact, good for students.

BIBLIOGRAPHY

Airasian, Peter W., Joseph F. Engemann, and Tiffany L. Gallagher. 2007. *Classroom assessment: Concepts and applications.* Toronto, ON: McGraw-Hill Ryerson.
This is a very good textbook on constructing and using a variety of assessment instruments.

Brookhart, Susan M. 2009. Assessment and examinations. In *International handbook of research on teachers and teaching,* ed. Lawrence J. Saha and A. Gary Dworking, 723–38. New York: Springer.
This excellent chapter carefully summarizes the principles of good classroom assessment.

Cirtwell, Charles, Rodney A. Clifton, and John D'Orsay. 2002. *Testing & accountability: The keys to educational excellence in Atlantic Canada.* Halifax, NS: Atlantic Institute for Market Studies.
This report presents strong arguments for using standardized tests in schools.

Holmes, Mark. 1993. *The educator's guide to student evaluation.* Toronto: OISE Press.
This book is directed at teachers, but it is also very helpful for parents in understanding the ways that teachers can assess the achievement of students accurately and fairly.

Kohn, Alfie. 2000. *The case against standardized testing: Raising the scores, ruining the schools.* Portsmouth, NH: Heinemann.
This book provides the common arguments against using standardized tests in schools.

Nichols, Sharon, and David Berliner. 2007. *Collateral damage: How high-stakes testing corrupts America's schools.* Cambridge, MA: Harvard Education Press.
The authors argue that high-stakes testing and other accountability systems undermine effective teaching.

Phelps, Richard P. 2003. *Kill the messenger: The war on standardized testing.* New Brunswick, NJ: Transaction.
This book counters Alfie Kohn's arguments and provides a strong rationale for using standardized tests.

Wiggins, Grant. 1990. The case for authentic assessment. *Practical Assessment, Research & Evaluation* 2 (2).
This article presents the case for "authentic assessment" by one of its leading advocates.

3

Students Need Discipline

PROLOGUE

As Brad and Heather Wright walked down the halls of Jefferson High School, they couldn't help feeling uncomfortable. Even though classes were in session, a number of students were loitering noisily in the hallway. Some of them wore T-shirts with obscene slogans, while others wore hats and hoods that made it almost impossible to see their faces. They could hear profane language as they were walking past the students. Considerable pushing and shoving was also evident.

Brad and Heather were in the school because their son, Kevin, was a Grade 10 student. Ever since enrolling at Jefferson two months ago, Kevin had complained to his parents that he was being bullied and that it was getting progressively worse. The Wrights thought that it was certainly time for something to be done about the situation, so they had an appointment to talk with the school's vice principal, Kathleen Gibson, who was responsible for handling school discipline.

After greeting them, Ms. Gibson asked Brad and Heather about their concerns. "Our son Kevin is being bullied to the point where he no longer feels safe coming to school," began Brad. "He said that he reported a number of episodes to his teachers, but nothing happened to correct the situation." After providing more details about the incidents, Brad exclaimed, "We regard this bullying as very serious and it must stop!"

Heather added, "These bullies need to be punished. They should be expelled from school if they don't smarten up and leave our son alone."

Up to this point, Ms. Gibson had listened patiently, but at the suggestion
of expelling students, she explained, "I understand that you are upset at how
some boys have treated your son. However, at Jefferson High School we believe that all students, including these boys, are valued members of our school
community. We have a formal discipline policy and you received a copy of it
when Kevin enrolled two months ago. Removing these boys from the school
may be an option, but only after proper investigation determines that Kevin
was, in fact, bullied by them."

Heather couldn't believe what she was hearing. "Are you saying," Heather
began incredulously, "that our son has reported these incidents to his teachers, but no one has yet investigated them?"

"We are still investigating Kevin's allegations, but we have not yet reached
a conclusion," replied Ms. Gibson.

"That's ridiculous!" interrupted Brad. "We're talking about bullying that
has gone on for over a month! Judging by what we saw and heard in the hallway, it doesn't seem you believe in discipline at all."

Ms. Gibson paused for a few seconds to catch her breath before responding. "I'm sorry you feel that way. As required by our discipline policy, all
students must be given due process. Also, we prefer restitution to punitive
discipline because we know that a focus on punishment simply does not work.
Don't you agree?"

"No, I don't," replied Brad. "Our son is suffering, doesn't want to come to
school, and no one here seems to care. Your investigation is simply taking too
long, and punishment is exactly what these bullies need."

Realizing that the conversation with Ms. Gibson was not going to satisfy
their concerns, at least not immediately, Brad and Heather left the vice principal's office in frustration. "Maybe we should send Kevin to another school,"
said Heather in exasperation as they walked to the parking lot.

Brad nodded in agreement. "It looks like we don't have much choice. If our
son isn't safe, we're not going to have him attend Jefferson. This school seems
to have so little discipline anyway. Why would we want him to stay?"

INTRODUCTION

What is wrong at Jefferson High School? Most people would have no difficulty identifying the immediate problem. Assuming that Kevin's reports of
bullying are correct, the school has failed to provide a timely and corrective

response to a very serious matter. Is there a more fundamental problem? Yes, very likely. Consider, for example, the Wrights' experience as they walked down the school hallway. Apparently, the teachers and administrators are ignoring offensive language and disruptive behavior by some students. Add to this the vice principal's inadequate response to the Wrights' concerns. Overall, it seems that the school has a poorly enforced discipline policy.

To the Wrights, the teachers and administrators are supporting a culture of indiscipline by indulgence and neglect; not only are disrespectful language and behavior tolerated by the teachers and administrators, but bullies are not brought to timely account. Obviously, the Wrights think that justice is not being served at Jefferson High. Many parents and teachers would probably agree that this school needs to tighten its discipline protocols, and that the teachers and administrators need to be serious about enforcing them.

WHAT IS THE PURPOSE OF SCHOOL DISCIPLINE ANYWAY?

Many educators believe that most discipline problems will take care of themselves if the curriculum and classroom teaching is sufficiently engaging. Some romantic progressive educators, most notably Alfie Kohn (2001), have even moved beyond this idea and attack any form of school discipline that relies on rewards and punishments because it emphasizes coercive compliance, which is not what parents, teachers, and administrators ultimately want. In fact, he claims that the problem is teachers who control students and make them conform to what they believe to be acceptable standards of behavior.

According to Kohn, "the more we manage students' behavior and try to make them do what we say, the more difficult it is for them to become morally sophisticated people who think for themselves and care about others" (Kohn 2001, 62). To achieve these objectives, Kohn thinks that schools should be democratic communities, not bureaucratic institutions, where students and teachers negotiate, more or less, the structure and limits on their behavior. Administrators following Kohn's advice will tend to focus on the coercive behavior of teachers and not on the behavior of students, presuming that students, set free from arbitrary rules and boring lessons, will naturally become inquisitive and well behaved.

We agree that an engaging curriculum and stimulating teachers will reduce discipline problems, and, of course, we agree that schooling should produce "morally sophisticated people who think for themselves and care about others." However, we find Kohn's idea of the school as a democracy unrealistic and his approach naive. The analysis and recommendations of Rodney Clifton and Lance Roberts (1993) in *Authority in Classrooms* are more persuasive than Kohn's approach.

Specifically, these writers examine the authority of teachers and the dynamics in schools that encourage or discourage students to comply with the expectations of teachers and administrators. Rejecting the image of the school as a democracy, Clifton and Roberts conclude that students who choose to violate commonsense rules of courtesy, respect, and safety in their relations with teachers and fellow students must accept appropriate consequences. For this reason, Kohn's advice is not helpful precisely because it trivializes the sensible belief of most parents, teachers, and administrators that courtesy, respect, and safety are necessary for socializing and educating young people to mature civility.

Accordingly, we believe that discipline policies in schools must be consistent with the distinctive social mandate of schooling. Ordinarily, this is understood as the establishment of rules of conduct to ensure that teaching and learning can be effectively accomplished, and that children and adolescents learn the essential ideas, skills, and dispositions that are necessary for functioning in a civil community—in the school, the neighborhood, and the wider society. In the interests of education and socialization, all students must be given the opportunity to learn and contribute something valuable, even those who are sometimes disrespectful of the rights and interests of others.

In well-managed schools, intelligent, corrective steps that attempt to promote personal responsibility for one's behavior—self-discipline—will always be necessary because schools deal with the growth and development of the young. This is simply common sense. James Q. Wilson (1993), for example, in *The Moral Sense*, says that a civil society is characterized by prudence, duty, courtesy, cooperation, and fairness. Given the social mandate of schools, self-respect and respect for the rights and interests of others must be at the center of any discipline policy.

THE BASIC PRINCIPLES OF DISCIPLINE

It is not our intention to establish detailed discipline policies for all schools. We recognize that the specific rules for a public high school in New York City may be different from those for a small village school in rural Saskatchewan.

Also, we know that teachers and administrators have a much better under-standing of their particular students, schools, and communities than we do. Therefore, we identify three basic principles that we think will support the establishment and maintenance of effective discipline in any school.

1. Educators Must Lead the Establishment of Disciplinary Rules to Ensure That They Are Appropriate, Clear, and Known

In the first instance, it is the responsibility of educators to take the lead in establishing discipline standards and protocols—the rules of discipline—that reflect the core values of a civil community. Moreover, teachers and adminis-trators—indeed all who work in the school—must be relentless in modeling and securing these values. Because rules are simply specific ways of giving expression to core values, the relationship between rules and values must be taught and demonstrated in schools.

Recall that Kohn and his supporters argue that the major problem in schools is the desire of teachers to be authority figures. Rather than the school establishing a set of rules at the beginning of the year, Kohn suggests that students need to be equally involved with their teachers and administrators in creating the rules throughout the year. In short, teachers need to empower students by giving them responsibilities in establishing the rules and the con-sequences that govern their behavior.

This prescription is unwise because it fails to acknowledge that the teachers—not the students—are professionally and legally responsible for ensuring that learning takes place in their classrooms and that the safety and well-be-ing of everyone is assured. To carry out these responsibilities, educators need to maintain control. In fact, teachers are employed to help students learn, and they have the fundamental responsibility to regulate their behavior in the interests of education and socialization. If teachers really are professionals, they need to accept fully their responsibilities for managing educational set-tings. A very important part of this responsibility is explaining and justifying discipline policies to students and their parents.

Teachers and administrators should not believe that students will naturally make good choices about learning so long as they are in a positive and sup-portive environment. After all, making good choices often calls for a certain amount of knowledge and experience, things that children don't always have. They may be well intentioned, but just mistaken or unaware of what constitutes good decisions. Certainly, a positive and supportive environment is something that educators must provide, but that, alone, is insufficient.

All students, no matter their ages, need clear policies and secure knowledge that the stated policies are the real policies and will be backed up with concrete action, fairly executed. In short, students need a structured and orderly environment to learn the values of civil society. What they do not need is the loose and indulgent environment that the Wrights encountered on their visit to Jefferson High, and they don't need administrators, like Ms. Gibson, who do not respond quickly to serious violations of the school's established code of conduct.

Most private schools, and increasingly some public schools in North America, expect students to wear uniforms and teachers to dress professionally, consistent with their responsibilities and status. Isn't it somewhat puzzling that the reasons for uniforms and dress codes in public schools have not been compelling? We think that such a requirement reflects clear expectations about the formal nature of the school, its serious social mandate, and the different roles of students and teachers. Thus, we see this practice in more public schools as good policy.

Notice that the uniforms worn by school sports teams and bands convey not only a clear sense of identity but also a sense of pride in the institution. Add to this the role that uniforms can play in minimizing the visual aspects of socioeconomic inequalities in schools, to say nothing of the practicality of uniforms as a cost-effective way of reducing a family's clothing expenditures. In short, school uniforms are an egalitarian representation of institutional membership.

No doubt, some students and parents will argue that students will lose their individual identity if they are required to wear uniforms. We understand this claim, but we think that an increase in school identity and pride would be a useful feature of school discipline and decorum. And frankly, some clothing worn by adolescents should not be allowed in schools because it undermines prudence and the respect that others deserve; it is a sign of indiscipline.

Even if schools do not have a uniform for students, every school should at least have clearly spelled out dress codes that reflect the seriousness of the formal learning environment. It may be a cliché to say that the clothing people wear reflects their mind-set and can affect their behavior, but it is true. Some public schools may have gone too far in accepting individual expression in the way students and teachers dress. At the end of the day, schools are important institutions of learning, and students and teachers should dress in a way that indicates that they are engaged in serious work and not on their day off or treating every day as a "dress down or color day."

2. Disciplinary Rules Must Be Consistently Enforced to Ensure Credibility and Fairness

Along with clear behavioral expectations comes the need for consistent enforcement of them, and meaningful consequences for misbehavior are absolutely necessary. Policy is what educators do as well as what they say it is. Clearly identified policies and guidelines are worthless without the teeth to back them up. If teachers and administrators are unwilling, inconsistent, or lax in enforcing the rules, or are stingy with praise, some students will exploit or abuse the situation.

Some educators, including Kohn, are critical of positive and negative reinforcements in teaching and discipline. In fact, Kohn asserts that teachers should not criticize students when they do something wrong or reward them when they do something right. In his view, praise is simply another example of an extrinsic inducement, and teachers who say "good job" are undermining efforts to have students internalize good behavior. Instead, teachers need to provide students with unconditional acceptance and empowerment.

For Kohn, all rewards and punishments should be eliminated because they undermine the desire of students to do the right thing for its own sake. But this confuses knowing or recognizing that the right or wrong thing has been done with the motivation for respecting the norms of proper conduct. And so here, Kohn turns a legitimate criticism of the misuse of rewards and punishments into an absolute, but unworkable, directive. He is correct when he notes that some children become too dependent upon extrinsic rewards, but he is not recommending that teachers temper their praise and criticism with common sense—he is advocating its complete elimination. This solution is hopelessly naive and obviously wrong.

So students rightly need to be praised when they have done good work or when they have acted in an appropriate manner. Conversely, students who engage in disrespectful behavior, such as bullying other students or undermining the authority of teachers, should not receive unconditional acceptance. Rather, teachers must assert that proper behavior is expected and negative consequences are necessary to reduce unacceptable behavior. If the behavior of students dramatically improves, why should teachers not praise them? We see nothing wrong with moderate praise; likewise, we see nothing wrong with reasonable reprimands or even sanctions to change the misbehavior of students.

Emily Sachar, a journalist, spent a year as a teacher at Walt Whitman Intermediate School in New York City. In *Shut Up and Let the Lady Teach: A Teacher's Year in a Public School* (Sachar 1991), she paints a picture of a school in almost complete chaos. Desks were regularly broken, fights frequently broke out among students, profanity was constantly used, and classrooms were in so much disarray that it was almost impossible for teachers to survive until the end of the day. Parents who read her book will wonder how anyone could possibly expect learning to take place in such an environment.

What is ironic is that Walt Whitman Intermediate School actually had excellent policies regarding student behavior. The policies stated, among other things, that students were expected to refrain from using profanity, must arrive for their classes on time, and must show respect to their teachers. However, Sachar discovered that while these rules were in the code of conduct, they were rarely, if ever, enforced. Students had to commit major offenses, such as bringing guns to school or openly selling drugs, before administrators would discipline them.

The problem with this approach is obvious. When minor offenses are ignored, offenders become emboldened and engage in more serious offenses more frequently. It is exceedingly rare for students who have committed major offenses, such as bullying and selling drugs, to not have previously committed minor offenses. When teachers and administrators fail to provide meaningful consequences for minor transgressions, they create a climate in which ignoring the rules becomes routine. In time, some students will progress to more serious offenses, and by that time the prescribed consequences will be relatively ineffective. Habits of incivility will already have been formed.

The "Broken Windows" approach to safe, orderly, and clean neighborhoods, developed by James Q. Wilson and George L. Kelling (1982), contains a very similar idea for establishing and maintaining effective discipline in schools. Basically, this approach to improving neighborhoods, which has been used successfully in New York City, builds on a simple principle: repair broken windows in a neighborhood as soon as you find them. Otherwise, broken windows that have not been repaired, like rules that have not been enforced, become a signal that no one cares about the community: breaking more windows—or rules—has no specific consequences. Wilson and Kelling argue that the "untended behavior" of breaking windows leads to the breakdown of feelings of mutual regard, trust, and cooperation, and the obligations of civility become severely attenuated. The result is that law-abiding citizens lose control of their neighborhood.

Applying to schools the principle that untended misbehavior seriously undermines the core norm of civility, we arrive at a very similar conclusion to that of Emily Sachar regarding the approach to discipline that would make any school a positive and successful environment for teaching and learning. In short, teachers and administrators need to care about the behavior of their students and the normative order of their classrooms and school so that appropriate behavior is reinforced and inappropriate behavior is not tolerated. This is one of the most effective ways to secure civility in schools. It is also one of the most challenging requirements for school teachers and administrators because without solidarity among teachers, administrators, and students, disciplinary rules and consequences will fail to achieve the educationally productive and civil environment that is everyone's goal.

And, of course, there is the important matter of fairness, specifically due process. It is a requirement of basic fairness that the facts of misbehavior must be properly ascertained, that explanations must be heard, that accounts must be treated judiciously, and that consequences must be applied evenly without malice. The message must be that misbehavior will not be tolerated because it jeopardizes core values of civility, and that the consequences are deserved and just.

3. Persistently Unruly Students Must Be Removed to Protect the Rights and Interests of Everyone

What should be done with students who deliberately sabotage the teacher's ability to teach, the opportunity of other students to learn, or the safety and well-being of others? Given our argument so far, the answer is obvious; they should be removed from the classroom or from the school until they no longer threaten the school's mission to educate and to assure the safety of teachers and students. Certainly, the rights of the students who want to learn must be considered more important than the rights of those who are unwilling to be constrained by the discipline policy.

In 1983, Joe Clark was appointed principal of Eastside High School in Paterson, New Jersey, with the mandate to turn around a school where disrespect, violence, drug dealing, and vandalism were rampant (Clark and Picard 1989). During his first week as principal, he identified the ringleaders and expelled approximately 10 percent of the three thousand students. His reason for expelling these students was that it was necessary to prevent anarchy from prevailing. In Clark's view, the school could not function properly with students whose sole purpose was to sell drugs, intimidate other students, and disrupt their learning.

Within two years, Eastside High School had made such a remarkable turnaround that it was declared a model school by the state governor. Clark's achievements were recognized in a feature story in *Time* magazine, and President Ronald Reagan offered him a job as an education policy advisor. The movie, *Lean on Me*, is closely modeled on Clark's success, and the film is inspirational in showing how a strong principal can turn a failing school into a successful one.

How many school administrators are willing to take the tough action that Clark took at Eastside High School? When teachers and principals act as if the rights of all students need to be equally respected, even those who bully other students or sell drugs, they are downplaying the education and well-being of others. In the prologue to this chapter, Kevin Wright was being bullied, and the vice principal, Kathleen Gibson, seemed unwilling to assure his safety and provide a timely investigation of the behavior of the alleged bullies. In such circumstances, we think it is basic common sense to start correcting the behavior of bullies, but if that is not possible, they must be removed from the school so that they do not threaten or disrupt the rights and interests of the students who want to learn.

Just as law-abiding citizens should have more freedom than criminals, the interests of hardworking and obedient students should take precedence over students who intentionally disrupt the learning environment. Hence schools cannot tolerate obnoxious behavior, disrespect, persistent mischief, belligerence, or hooliganism by students, and suspension from the classroom and expulsion from the school must be available as disciplinary measures.

RECOMMENDATIONS

First, all schools must have clear discipline policies that identify expectations, consequences of misbehavior, and the protocols that govern disciplinary matters, including due process, and parental notification of misdeeds and their consequences. It is important that the discipline policies, with all relevant details, be communicated to students, parents, and the community. It is wise for school boards to ensure that common principles of discipline inform all school rules within their jurisdiction, especially those regarding due process.

In addition, principals must have the authority to remove unruly students from the school to safeguard the learning environment. Obviously, reasonable efforts should be made to educate students who are difficult to handle, but it should never be at the expense of students who want to learn. Students who are removed should not be allowed to re-enter the classroom or the school until they have reformed their behavior.

Second, it is important for students to receive a consistent message from their home, school, and community. As such, parents must ensure that their children understand the importance of good behavior at school, and children must understand that their parents will support the disciplinary practices of teachers and principals that are consistent with the formal policy. And parents should not defend their children against teachers and principals when their children are clearly at fault.

Finally, schools of education that are responsible for training teachers need to be very serious about the effective management of classrooms and schools. All prospective teachers need to receive solid instruction in ways of establishing discipline and they must be able to demonstrate their capacity to do this prior to being certified as full-fledged teachers. Obviously, students need discipline, and clear behavioral expectations, specific consequences for misbehavior, consistent enforcement, and no tolerance for persistently unruly students are essential for effective discipline in schools, which is, of course, necessary for effective teaching and learning.

BIBLIOGRAPHY

Charles, C. M. 2008. *Building classroom discipline*. Boston: Pearson Education.
   The objective of this book is to help teachers develop their own personal systems of discipline tailored to their philosophies and personalities, as well as the needs of their school and community.

Clark, Joe L., with Joe Picard. 1989. *Laying down the law: Joe Clark's strategy for saving our schools.* Washington, DC: Regnery Publishing.
This is a fascinating book in which Joe Clark describes his experience in overcoming serious discipline problems as principal of Eastside High School.

Clifton, Rodney A., and Lance W. Roberts. 1993. *Authority in classrooms.* Scarborough, ON: Prentice Hall.
This book explains the rationale for the authority of teachers and describes how teachers and administrators need to cooperate to maintain effective discipline in their classrooms and schools.

Kohn, Alfie. 2001. *Beyond discipline: From defiance to community.* Upper Saddle River, NJ: Merrill/Prentice Hall.
Alfie Kohn argues for granting students almost unlimited autonomy because he thinks that schools must be democratic institutions.

Sachar, Emily. 1991. *Shut up and let the lady teach: A teacher's year in a public school.* New York: Simon & Schuster.
This book provides a candid description of Emily Sachar's disturbing experience of teaching in an inner-city school in New York City.

Wilson, James Q. 1993. *The moral sense.* New York: The Free Press.
This outstanding book examines the moral basis of civil society and explains why human nature cannot be discounted by those who want institutions, like schools, to function effectively.

Wilson, James Q., and George L. Kelling. 1982. "Broken windows: The police and neighborhood safety." *Atlantic Monthly* (March): 29–37.
This article argues that law-abiding citizens must not tolerate minor offenses lest they send the message that no one cares about the well-being of the community.

4

Inclusion Should Not
Be Exclusion

PROLOGUE

Katherine Smith was being kept busy by her twenty-six Grade 4 students. She had just finished presenting a lesson about converting fractions into decimals and had assigned a fifteen-question worksheet for the students to complete before the recess bell rang. As Katherine walked around the room, she saw that, as usual, some students were having much more difficulty with the questions than others.

"Miss Smith," called out Robbie. "I don't understand how to do these questions." After spending several minutes showing Robbie how to convert fractions into decimals for the second time, she realized that he was overwhelmed with the number of questions in the assignment.

"Okay, Robbie," explained Katherine. "See if you can do at least the first five questions. That's all you need to do before we go over the answers tomorrow." Robbie seemed to feel better and said he would do his best.

After dealing with Robbie, Katherine went to the next student with her hand up. "I'm done the assignment, Miss Smith," said Amber, "What should I do now?" Katherine took a look at her worksheet and saw that all the questions were indeed completed and they all looked as though they were correct.

"How about reading a book for the rest of the period?" suggested Katherine. Amber sighed and seemed disappointed that there was nothing else to do in math. With half an hour to go before recess, Amber knew that this was going to be a rather long wait. She could probably finish the last thirty pages in the novel she was reading.

At that moment Katherine heard a loud groan from the back of the classroom. Bertha, a wheelchair-bound student with the mental capacity of a five-year-old, was having another seizure. Her teaching assistant (TA) was expert in helping Bertha, but it took several minutes to get Bertha to stop groaning and to open her eyes. During this time, the other students were distracted and not working on their math sheets. Katherine circled the room trying to get the students focused on completing the worksheet while the TA settled Bertha down.

After this disruption, Katherine resumed her walk around the room, seeing how the students were doing. Frank put up his hand, and as she walked over to his desk Katherine noticed that he was still working on the math booklet he had received from the resource teacher. The booklet contained modified math questions at a Grade 1 level, but they were too difficult for Frank. Katherine again found herself explaining to Frank how to add one single-digit number to another single-digit number. While it was clear that he still didn't understand the procedure no matter how carefully she explained it, he was able to get a few more questions completed when she helped him.

Katherine was quite relieved to hear the recess bell ring at the end of the period. As her students rushed out of the room, she thought about her experiences in the math lesson. "I can't believe how diverse my students really are. I have students like Amber who find the work too easy and could probably be in Grade 6, and I also have extremely weak students, like Frank and Robbie, who understand very little of my lessons and are so dependent on me. And then there's Bertha. I'm not sure that she's even aware of where she is," thought Katherine to herself.

Katherine looked at the clock and realized that she only had a few minutes left to get ready for science before the students would be back in the classroom after recess. Again, Katherine thought to herself, "It sure would be nice if I could just teach a single lesson without having to adapt and modify it for students at so many different levels. I spend most of my time helping the weak students understand what they are required to do. I guess that I'll never have the luxury of teaching and evaluating students who have similar abilities."

INTRODUCTION

Katherine's experience is not uncommon. Walk into almost any public school in North America and you will find classrooms where some students are working well above their grade level while others, who have learning disabilities or social and behavioral disorders that affect their school progress, are working below their grade level. In addition, you will see students with such severe physical, sensory, or behavioral disabilities that they require full-time teacher assistants (TAs) even when they are not participating in any of the classroom activities. Somehow, teachers are supposed to design and implement programs that meet the needs of all these students.

This is the world of "mainstreaming" or "inclusion," a policy of student placement where virtually all students are assigned to regular classrooms even when some of them have disabilities so severe that they cannot participate in what are considered routine or normal activities. It is the norm, rather than the exception, for teachers to have students in their classrooms whose differences in ability and proficiency are considerable. For example, a Grade 6 teacher may have some students working at the Grade 4 level and a few who are working well beyond the Grade 6 level.

In the past, the situation was quite different. Specifically, severely disabled students were often educated in separate classrooms or in separate schools or hospitals. Even for students who were considered to be in the normal range of ability, grouping or "streaming" on the basis of their ability and performances was common. Students were grouped into classrooms with other students at similar levels, and consequently all students could generally understand what was being taught the first time, and the teacher did not need to prepare separate lessons for students at various levels. Even today school clubs, such as badminton, chess, and debating are usually organized so that students compete against others who have similar proficiencies.

However, streaming, or separating children into classroom groups of similar performance levels, has become an anathema for many romantic progressives; it runs counter to the prevailing philosophy of inclusion. Those who advocate inclusion generally support keeping academically weak and severely disabled students in regular classrooms, arguing that all students benefit from having disabled students in regular classrooms because the diversity promotes tolerance, acceptance, and understanding. They believe that greater classroom diversity and the promotion of tolerance constitute worthy educational outcomes.

In short, keeping students of varying ability levels together—heterogeneous grouping—is considered to be a better approach than grouping students homogeneously on the basis of similar abilities and/or performances.

EVALUATING MAINSTREAMING

While we are not in favor of rigid streaming, we believe that the pendulum of educational philosophy and practice has swung too far in the direction of mainstreaming severely disabled students, ignoring common sense and what is reasonable to expect from teachers. To ask classroom teachers to design and implement engaging and effective programs of instruction for twenty-five to thirty students with widely different levels of ability and performance, even if they have teaching assistants to help them, is more problematic than many administrators and parents seem to realize.

Sometimes it is so challenging for teachers that it is unrealistic. It sets teachers up for failure because it requires them to modify their teaching and curricular goals and try to teach students with substantial differences in skills and knowledge. Their time, energy, and attention are hopelessly divided in an effort to make their instruction and evaluation appropriate to the variability among their students. At worst, the care and accommodation of some severely disabled children in regular classrooms is very distracting and disruptive for both teachers and other students.

From this perspective, mainstreaming may be unfair to all students and not only unfair for those at the extremes of performance. Specifically, this strategy can fail to provide adequate challenges for gifted students and it can disadvantage the weakest students because the teacher's instruction and support are insufficient. Some students with severe disabilities are not even aware of their surroundings, and having them in the classroom creates the false impression that they are receiving an education equal to that received by the other students.

Realistically, we should ask: would these children be better served if they were cared for and educated in separate, more specialized classrooms, where programs of instruction and support could be more carefully adapted to their circumstances, abilities, and needs? Most recently, Daniel Hallahan and others (2010, 31), in their book *Exceptional Learners*, note that it is a myth that "research has established beyond a doubt that special classes are ineffective and that mainstreaming is effective"; rather, they say that the "research comparing special versus mainstream placements has been inconclusive."

In light of the question posed in the preceding paragraph, we ask: why has mainstreaming become the predominant placement strategy in most North American public schools? There are a number of reasons for the popularity of this strategy, but perhaps the main factor has been legislative mandates and legal entitlements that have emerged from case law concerning the rights of disabled children and their parents. This public policy development began in the mid-1970s in the United States and about a decade later in Canada. Along with emerging expectations of egalitarianism, parents, educators, and governmental agencies increasingly viewed the public school as the primary agency for promoting greater social equality.

We support the promotion of both social equality and tolerance as legitimate educational aims, but we question the educational effectiveness of the inclusion of all disabled students regardless of their needs, abilities, and interests. Where feasible, and depending on the nature of the particular disability, disabled students should be in regular classrooms. Just because students are in wheelchairs does not mean they should be excluded. Wheelchair ramps and elevators can readily compensate for students with some disabilities. And, students with poor vision can be provided with special glasses and large-print books that make it possible for them to function successfully alongside their classmates. But, deafness or blindness, for example, results in teachers having more difficulty adapting their instruction, evaluation, and safety procedures.

Of course, modifications can help to minimize the difficulties posed by particular disabilities, but they do not necessarily eliminate them. What possible advantage does a fourteen-year-old boy with the mental capacity of a five-year-old gain from being in a Grade 9 classroom? Surely this is misplaced egalitarianism that cannot be realistically defended on the basis of educational or social benefits. Here, the principle of inclusivity is overriding the more basic principle that teaching be adapted to the child's ability, performance, and needs. Students with severe disabilities usually need expert care and specialized instruction that cannot easily be provided by regular teachers in regular classrooms.

This principle of accommodation was articulated in *Eaton v. Brant* (1997) by the Supreme Court of Canada, where the Court provided an interpretation of the legal rights of a multiple-handicapped student under the equality clause of the *Canadian Charter of Rights and Freedoms*, Canada's constitutional bill of rights. Emily Eaton was a severely handicapped ten-year-old child with cerebral palsy who could not speak, had no other mode of communication, was visually impaired, and was confined to a wheelchair.

After two years, during which she was in Kindergarten and Grade 1, the Brant County Board of Education in Ontario decided that she should be placed in a segregated, special-education classroom in another school. Significantly, her teachers recommended Emily's special placement because they believed that she was neither educationally nor socially advantaged by being integrated into a regular classroom. However, Emily's parents resisted this decision and insisted that she be placed in a regular classroom.

Following an appeal to a Special Education Tribunal and a judicial review in the lower courts, the Supreme Court ruled that Emily's constitutional right to equality—the right to equal protection and benefit of the law and a right not to be discriminated against on the basis of "mental or physical disability"—had *not* been violated by the decision of the school board. The Court observed that the parents' view of their child's best interest was inadequate and that the Special Education Tribunal had "balanced the various educational interests of Emily Eaton, taking into account her special needs, and concluded that the best possible placement was in the special class . . . it seems incongruous that a decision reached after such an approach could be considered a burden or a disadvantage imposed on a child" (409).

Specifically, the Court reasoned that the test of the child's best interest should not be encumbered by a presumption in favor of integration and that the test of equality was not necessarily access to a regular classroom but rather the failure to make reasonable accommodation to the real abilities and needs of the disabled person. The Court explained its ruling in a careful statement of principle:

> [S]egregation can be both protective of equality and violative of equality depending upon the person and the state of disability. In some cases, special education is a necessary adaptation of the mainstream world which enables some disabled pupils access to the learning environment they need in order to have an equal opportunity in education. While integration should be recognized as the norm of general application because of the benefits it generally provides, a presumption in favour of integrated schooling would work to the disadvantage of pupils who require special education in order to achieve equality. Schools focused on the needs of the blind or deaf, and special education for students with learning disabilities, indicate the positive aspects of segregated education placement. Integration can be either a benefit or a burden depending on whether the individual can profit from the advantages that integration provides. (406–7)

As yet, no strict parallel of this judicial ruling has been articulated by the United States Supreme Court, likely because of the extensive provisions of Public Law 94-142, *Education for All Handicapped Children Act* (1975), Section 504 of the *Rehabilitation Act* (1973), and the *Americans with Disabilities Act* (1990). These U.S. federal statutes overshadow all others at the federal level that relate to the education of the disabled. There is no Canadian federal legislation that is parallel in scope and content.

The U.S. federal statute, *Education for All Handicapped Children Act*, has since 1975 regulated the approval of state plans for educating handicapped students and includes "the right to a free and appropriate public education and the right to placement in the least restrictive environment, insofar as possible, with non-handicapped children, and whenever possible, at the same school they would attend if they were not handicapped." Thus, a central issue for the courts in the United States has been the interpretation of "appropriate education" in specific cases. Since parents and schools do not always agree on the educational placement or programs that are appropriate for a particular disabled child, American jurisprudence repeatedly reveals the inherent tension in interpreting these words.

For example, in *Lachman v. Illinois Board of Education* (1988), a school district proposed to place a seven-year-old deaf student in a self-contained classroom for hearing-impaired students for at least one-half of the school day. The child's parents objected and asked that their child be placed in a regular classroom with the assistance of a full-time speech instructor. Eventually, the dispute was referred to the Illinois Appeals Court, which ruled in favor of the school district, noting that the preference for mainstreaming in the federal legislation "must be balanced against the possibility that some students could be better educated in segregated facilities" (O'Reilly and Green 1992, 148).

Moreover, in *Greer v. Rowe City School District* (1991), a circuit court ruled that if a child's behavior significantly disrupts the education of the other children, then placing that child in a regular classroom could properly be judged as inappropriate. Nevertheless, the court observed that the requirement of extra attention by the teacher to meet the specific needs of a disabled child is not, alone, a sufficient reason to place such a child in a segregated classroom. This conclusion does not seem to take account of the severity of a disability, the extra attention required to manage the child in the classroom, or the number of other disabled students in the classroom with a single teacher. For this reason, some educators and parents will certainly find this judicial assessment troublesome.

Given the complexity of these court decisions, it is easy to see that no single court ruling is likely to end a long-standing and often very emotional debate on the disabled child's rights to equality and an appropriate education, either in Canada or in the United States. But the courts have not been entirely unhelpful; they have clarified certain legal principles and unraveled a number of dilemmas in the placement of disabled students: (1) the most appropriate education is not necessarily in the least restrictive environment; (2) the most inclusive classroom is not necessarily the most appropriate program; and (3) the least restrictive classroom is not necessarily the most supportive one. In short, the real possibility is that the most enabling classrooms for some disabled children may well be specialized programs in segregated classrooms, at least for a substantial portion of their school lives.

In the current educational climate, we think that the most serious risk to equal opportunity for disabled students lies in the overly enthusiastic support for the principle of inclusivity, either by a school system, by parents, or both. As a prescriptive norm for the placement of all school-aged children, inclusion may fail to recognize that some students may be excluded from the type of instruction and care that will help them most.

In fact, severely disabled students are being placed in regular classrooms where they are integrated only in their physical presence and not in their participation in the classroom learning, where disruption is often evident, and where isolation from other students is not uncommon. Are schools doing this because of an uncritical application of the reigning ideology—the inclusion of all children in mainstream classrooms, irrespective of their specific abilities and needs? Cannot common sense be used in placement decisions regarding severely disabled students?

Obviously, many academically weak students recognize their own difficulties when they are in classrooms where most of the other students are ahead of them. And strong students are sometimes prevented from progressing at a pace that challenges them because their right to an appropriate education is considered, even by some educators, to be less important because they are gifted and it is assumed that they can cope on their own. Moreover, excellent teachers experience considerable frustration and despair with the wide variability of knowledge, skills, and proficiencies of the students in their classrooms.

It is obviously time to ask: What implications for teaching, learning, and school administration flow from policies of mainstreaming and appropriate education? How do we ensure that inclusion does not mean exclusion or the creation of disadvantage for some students, including those who are most able?

RECOMMENDATIONS

We are not advocating a wholesale return to streaming students into classrooms on the basis of a narrow range of abilities and performances in the early grades. Students need to be with others who are different from them, which requires that they work with students who have different levels of ability and different interests. This is a reality that is both desirable and acceptable within a reasonable range for most classrooms and most teachers.

Of course, judging the reasonableness of the range of students' abilities depends on the specific teacher and students in a classroom; some teachers and students can work effectively with greater variability in their classrooms than other teachers and students. But presently, we think that the pendulum of educational practice has swung too far in the direction of mainstreaming; the practice has become too rigid and inflexible, creating situations that are unreasonable for many students and teachers.

First, we suggest that school districts approach implementing mainstreaming and appropriate education policies with considerable caution. Most notably, students with severe disabilities who cannot function in regular classrooms should be provided with specialized programs of instruction, at least for a portion of the day. Policies that require school administrators to place extremely disabled students in regular classrooms risk placing an unfair burden on those students, other students, and on their teachers.

We are not saying that teachers should never be expected to provide for differences in their students' abilities and interests. Many teachers, for example, group students who have similar reading levels and spend focused time helping them learn material at their level of proficiency. It is interesting that many of the most successful teaching strategies in classrooms involve putting students into similar ability-level groups. But this practice begs the question: why is it acceptable for teachers to divide their students into different reading groups but unacceptable for principals to group students into different classes so that each teacher has a narrower range of students to teach and supervise?

Arguably, language and mathematics are two of the most important skills for school success, and we recommend using proficiency in reading, comprehension, writing, and mathematical skills in the placement of students. If a school is large enough to have more than one classroom per grade, we see nothing wrong with grouping students into separate classrooms based on their achievement levels. This policy would undoubtedly increase the variability in age among students, but it would reduce the variability in knowledge and skills within classrooms. It certainly would make teaching simpler and more effective because it would be easier for teachers to design lessons that challenge all of the students. In short, common sense ought to prevail.

Most fundamentally, we support providing equal educational opportunities for all students, but not at the expense of excellence—excellence in the form of the best and most appropriate setting and resources for all students. For this to happen, however, there needs to be a fundamental shift in philosophy in schools of education and in provincial and state departments of education.

Too many educators and administrators in these institutions seem to believe that equality is more important than excellence. We need to pay at least as much attention to the gifted students as we currently pay to the weaker students. As Charles Murray (2008) eloquently explains in *Real Education*, a nation that fails to properly educate its gifted students jeopardizes its future.

BIBLIOGRAPHY

Agne, Karen. 1998. The dismantling of the great American public school.
    Educational Horizons (Spring): 127–31.
    Karen Agne identifies many of the difficulties caused by mainstreaming all
    students in public schools and notes how this policy has led to the exodus of some
    students to private schools and home schooling.

Eaton v. Brant (County) Board of Education (1997). 142 D. L. R. (4th) 385.
    In this decision, the Supreme Court of Canada ruled that placing disabled
    students in regular classrooms is not necessarily in their best interest if their
    particular disabilities cannot be adequately addressed in that setting.

Endepohls-Ulpe, Martina. 2009. Teaching gifted and talented children. In
    International handbook of research on teachers and teaching, ed. Lawrence J. Saha
    and A. Gary Dworking, 881–94. New York: Springer.
    This chapter defines giftedness, summarizes the educational needs of gifted
    children, and identifies the type of programs that can be provided for them.

Fischer, Louis, David Schimmel, and Leslie R. Stelman. 2003. *Teachers and the law.* Boston: Pearson Education.

This is a clearly written book that outlines the many legal issues that are seriously affecting the work of both teachers and administrators. The authors use common language that is easily understood by teachers, principals, and parents.

Greer v. Rowe City School District, 950 F 2d 688 (11th Cir. 1991).

This decision allows for the separate placement of disabled children where their presence significantly impairs the education of the other children. This legal decision also notes that the requirement of extra attention by the teacher to meet the specific needs of disabled students is not, alone, a sufficient reason to place them in segregated classrooms.

Hallahan, Daniel P., James M. Kauffman, Laureen J. McIntyre, and David Mykota. 2010. *Exceptional learners: An introduction to special education.* Toronto: Pearson Canada.

This is a good introductory textbook on the characteristics of exceptional learners, those children whose ability and performance are outside the normal range; that is, children with physical, sensory, and learning disabilities, and also those who are considered gifted. It discusses and evaluates current trends, issues, and practices, and includes a comprehensive description of "responsive instruction" for the full range of exceptionalities.

Knight, Bruce A. 2009. Teaching students with special needs. In *International handbook of research on teachers and teaching,* ed. Lawrence J. Saha and A. Gary Dworking, 865–79. New York: Springer.

This chapter summarizes the philosophy, government policies, and problems of including students with special needs in regular classrooms.

Lachman v. Illinois Board of Education, 852 F 2d (7th Cir. 1988).

In this decision, the Illinois Appeals Court ruled that the preference for mainstreaming in federal legislation "must be balanced against the possibility that some students could be better educated in segregated facilities."

MacKay, A. Wayne, and Lyle Sutherland. 2006. *Teachers and the law* (2nd ed.). Toronto: Emond Montgomery.

This book reviews the case law in education that has emerged over the twenty-five years since the *Canadian Charter of Rights and Freedoms* was enacted. The authors show that Canadian educational policy makers, administrators, and teachers must navigate increasingly complex legal judgments that affect their work.

Murray, Charles. 2008. *Real education: Four simple truths for bringing America's schools back to reality.* New York: Crown Forum.
This groundbreaking book challenges a number of the premises upon which the education system in North America is based. Most importantly, Murray shows how excellence in American education is being sacrificed in the name of equality.

O'Reilly, Robert C., and Edward T. Green. 1992. *School law for the 1990s: A handbook.* New York: Greenwood Press.
This handbook provides a comprehensive examination of the realities in which teachers and administrators in American public schools must function.

Shanker, Albert. 1995. Full inclusion is neither free nor appropriate. *Educational Leadership* 52 (December/January): 18–21.
Former president of the American Federation of Teachers Albert Shanker provides a strong critique of the policy of mainstreaming virtually all students. He points out that many teachers will have serious difficulties in fulfilling the mandate.

Thernstrom, Abigail. 1999. Courting disorder in the schools. *Public Interest* 136:18–34.
This article examines the legal reasons for mainstreaming exceptional students in the United States, and notes the serious practical problems that result for both students and teachers. The author notes that the mainstreaming policy has often made school discipline a "nightmare" for teachers and administrators.

Villa, Richard A., and Jacqueline S. Thousand. 2003. Making inclusive education work. *Educational Leadership* 61 (October): 19–23.
Villa and Thousand review the *Educational for All Handicapped Children Act* of 1975, which required schools to provide appropriate education to all students, especially those with disabilities, and they recommend a number of strategies that teachers and principals need to implement to fulfill this mandate.

5

Some Teachers Are Better Than Others

PROLOGUE

It was the third week of September and Michelle Bean and Janice Zaker, two mothers in their mid-thirties, had just bumped into each other at the local supermarket and begun chatting about how their children were doing. Since their daughters were in the same Grade 3 class, the discussion quickly focused on their daughters' new teacher and how pleased they were with her. "Boy, what a great teacher Jenni McLean is!" exclaimed Michelle.

"Yes, I agree, she has tons of energy, so much enthusiasm, and lots of good ideas about teaching!" replied Janice.

Before the first day of school, Jenni McLean invited all the parents to a meeting at the school so that she could get to know them. She arranged to have the principal and a caretaker in the school at 7:00 p.m. on the day before school began. The school was specifically opened for the parents, but there were a few other teachers in their classrooms preparing for the upcoming year. After greeting the parents, Jenni outlined what she was going to do with the children during the school year. The hour-long session was very well organized, and Jenni had already memorized the names of the twenty-five children who were going to be in her classroom.

Both women were very impressed with this beginning teacher. And, of course, they were very happy that their girls were excited about going to school this year.

"Do you have time for a coffee?" asked Janice.

"Okay," said Michelle as she turned toward the coffee kiosk in the store.

"Look at this," said Janice, as she picked up the folded newspaper from the table. The story headline on section B1 had caught her attention: "School Superintendent Defends Merit Pay Plan for Teachers." According to the story, the teachers' union was opposed to the plan and was vigorously fighting it, calling it an assault on the professionalism of teachers.

"I don't understand why this proposal is so controversial. Sure, teachers would need some assurances about the fairness of any evaluation, but all of us who work have our performance assessed by our supervisors. Why not pay excellent teachers more?" asked Michelle. "The teacher our girls had last year was terrible; she was disorganized, harsh, not really interested in teaching, and she wouldn't talk to parents except when the principal required it. Why did we have to put up with that? She should have been fired."

"Thank goodness she moved to another school, but I pity the poor kids who have her this year," replied Janice. "Good thing we have a great teacher or I would be sending Jennifer to another school, maybe a charter school or even a private school. We may be lucky, but those other parents are not. I don't understand why any principal, parents, or students should have to put up with that teacher."

"What do you think makes someone a good teacher, Janice?" asked Michelle.

After thinking for a moment, Janice replied, "Well, most important, I think that good teachers must like children and they must like working with them, even when it is hard work. Second, I think excellent teachers need to be smart; they need to know the curriculum and they need to know how to make it interesting for students."

"Do you think that excellent teachers need to challenge kids to do more, as Jennifer's swimming coach does?" asked Michelle. "And isn't it important for teachers to have enthusiasm and to be well organized, as Jenni McLean is?"

"Yes, of course teachers must be enthusiastic. They must like their students, and the subjects they teach so the children catch that interest from them. Good teachers need to challenge their kids and they need to evaluate them as often as her swimming coach does. And, yes, excellent teachers are well organized, like Jenni," replied Janice. After thinking for a moment she added, "There must be a few more skills that excellent teachers possess, but I think these are the most important ones that separate them from the poor teachers."

INTRODUCTION

In one short conversation, these two mothers who care deeply about their children have, in fact, identified some of the most important characteristics of effective teachers. This shouldn't be surprising since most parents of school-aged children have little difficulty telling the difference between good and bad teachers. But, making sure their children are in classrooms with highly effective teachers is usually more difficult. Of course, it would be ideal if all students had exemplary or excellent teachers, but many of us would be satisfied with all students having at least very good teachers, that is, those who are consistently effective in promoting academic achievement and sustaining the interest and motivation of students to study and learn.

Skeptics of the idea that effective teaching can be defined often claim that it's easy to be a good teacher in a school where most of the students come from stable, supportive, middle-class homes and where they are well fed and cared for. However, many teachers work in schools where most students are fortunate if they get one good meal a day.

Some argue that these teaching situations are so different that it is impossible to distinguish effective teachers from ineffective ones. In other words, some people believe that student performance is so connected to socioeconomic status and family background that the quality of teaching doesn't have any measurable effects on the academic achievement of students. We think this belief is wrong, and the research literature supports our judgment.

WHAT MAKES AN EFFECTIVE TEACHER?

For most parents, it is common sense to recognize that some teachers are better than others. Most parents know that teachers can't force students to learn, but effective teachers can manage twenty-five to thirty rambunctious youngsters, and they are able to organize their instruction so that students are very likely to learn the subject matter and acquire the necessary skills. While we cannot identify all the characteristics of effective teachers, it is possible to identify the most important attributes and skills that these teachers possess.

In *Qualities of Effective Teachers*, James Stronge (2002) summarizes the research on teacher effectiveness and produces a comprehensive inventory of these attributes and skills. He notes that a teacher who "has had solid educational preparation through course work and professional development" draws "on a multitude of skills and attributes in different combinations and different contexts to produce the results that define effectiveness" (64). In his summary of the evidence, Stronge (2002) shows that effective teachers exhibit a combination of personal and professional attributes, organizational skills, instructional skills, and use specific evaluation procedures in their teaching.

1. Personal and Professional Attributes

Effective teachers are empathetic toward their students and they have an interest and concern about their students' lives in and out of school. Also, effective teachers treat their students with respect and fairness, irrespective of their social background. In their interaction with students they are active listeners, friendly, yet maintain a professional disposition.

Effective teachers are also enthusiastic and take pleasure in the subjects they teach; they maintain high quality work, they accept responsibility for student outcomes, and they systematically use reflection to improve their teaching and their students' performances. Notably, effective teachers demonstrate a strong dedication to teaching, actively seek professional growth, and possess positive attitudes about their lives and work.

2. Organizational Skills

Basically, there are three aspects of being organized that effective teachers emphasize. The first concerns the arrangement of the classroom, the organization of routines, lesson materials, and administrative tasks, which are prepared in advance, yet anticipate necessary changes to accommodate new circumstances. Second, effective teachers give a high priority to sustaining students' attention and managing students by establishing rules of discipline, implementing them consistently and fairly, and stressing student responsibility for positive behavior. Also, these teachers anticipate potential problems and balance variety and challenge in their students' educational activities. Finally, effective teachers orchestrate smooth transitions and limit disruptions in their teaching and learning activities.

3. Instructional Skills

Obviously, effective teachers focus their classroom time on teaching and learning, and they maintain classroom momentum within and across lessons. They carefully link learning objectives and students' activities. They set clear, high expectations for themselves and for their students, and stress students' responsibilities and accountability. The planning of effective teachers reflects the attention spans and learning styles of their students, and they organize the content of their lessons for effective presentations.

Effective teachers also employ a wide repertoire of instructional strategies and techniques, orienting the students' experience toward improvement, and they give clear examples and guided practice to students. They know their subject matter well, and stress meaningful conceptualizations that reflect higher levels of cognitive understanding. Their questioning and assignments reflects the content to be mastered, and they emphasize literacy, reading, and mathematical skills. Effective teachers prize student engagement, and they lead, direct, and pace their students' learning activities.

4. Evaluation Procedures

Effective teachers monitor the progress of all their students carefully, giving clear, specific, and timely feedback, and, if necessary, reteaching and providing tutorial assistance to the students who are having difficulties. They suit their instruction and tutoring to the students' ability, achievement, needs, and interests, and they are alert to students' misconceptions. Effective teachers assign homework and set tests that clearly relate to the knowledge and skills that have been taught, and they review assignments and tests in class.

The distillation of the research literature by Stronge (2002) remarkably captures what some teachers, administrators, and professors of education consider an elusive phenomenon. We think that his book is a trustworthy guide for teachers, school administrators, parents, and professors of education. Along with Elaine McEwan (2002), Stronge (2002) shows that teaching effectiveness is not based on one aspect of skillful practice, but develops from a number of personal and professional attributes and skills.

For Stronge, the possession of these attributes and skills is still not enough; however, "the ultimate proof of teacher effectiveness is student results. The student should be able to read better, compute math more accurately, demonstrate a better understanding of her place in the world, or show other worthy achievements. In other words, measuring teacher success merely by teaching process is not enough; outcomes count" (65). We agree that academic achievement is crucial.

ARISTOTLE'S PRINCIPLES OF EFFECTIVE TEACHING

It is interesting to compare the characteristics of effective teachers that emerge from the modern research literature with the principles of good teaching that Aristotle identified 2,500 years ago (see Bredemeier and Bredemeier 1978, 318–22). Aristotle thought that good teachers needed to do three important things: convince students that their education is important, challenge them to understand the subject matter, and organize instruction so that students could grasp the ideas properly and think or perform competently. Obviously, Stronge (2002) would not be surprised by the idea that good teachers help their students understand that the subjects they are studying are important and useful.

The way this is done will vary with the subject matter, the teacher, and the age and maturity of their students. Effective teachers use a variety of well-established strategies to help students understand the importance of the subject matter. For young students, subject matter is generally presented as being useful, but older students need to be persuaded that abstract knowledge is important and that immediate relevance or practicality is not always the test of what is valuable. So, effective teachers help their students, even those who are having difficulty, to see how their classroom activities are important for their own success in school and society.

Once students are convinced that their school work is important, teachers must organize the material so that the students can master it. Effective teachers expect their students to be challenged by their attempt to understand the material at increasingly more complex levels. As students become more proficient, the challenges need to increase so that they experience some dissatisfaction, but not total frustration, with their present understanding, and as a result they recognize the necessity of improving their understanding. If students are not challenged, they are unlikely to learn new material and develop new skills.

Poor teachers often set objectives that are either too low or too high for their students. If the objectives are set too low, the students become bored; if they are set too high, the students become frustrated. For this reason, good teachers set objectives that are beyond the students' current understanding, but not so high that they do not have a good chance of achieving them. In addition, good teachers know what to do when their students have difficulties; they balance their expectations with their students' performances so that their expectations remain slightly ahead of the students' understanding to produce growth in understanding. When done properly, the process of setting challenging objectives, and having students achieve them, can give students a real and deserved sense of accomplishment as they learn to understand increasingly more complex ideas and master more advanced skills.

Finally, effective teachers understand that students need to have a sense of accomplishment to remain motivated. For this reason, effective teachers recognize the students' accomplishments with praise, and provide specific correction, assistance, and directions for improvement. Good teachers know that mastery does not always result from the initial attempts at learning something new, but can be achieved with persistent practice and dedicated work over a period of time. Obviously, some students need more time and assistance than others. The objective, of course, is to have the knowledge and skills eventually become integral to the students' confident grasp of the subject matter.

Aristotle's ideas suggest that good teaching is a combination of persuasion, "let me explain why learning this is good and useful for you;" challenge, "you might find this difficult at first but you can do it if you try hard;" and support, "I'll teach you what you need to know and I'll help you when you have difficulty." As Rodney Clifton and Lance Roberts (1993) point out, in a different conceptualization, effective teachers are active "warm demanders." These are the teachers who create a learning environment that is supportive and encouraging but who equally require students to become actively engaged in developing a better understanding of the subject matter.

This perspective resonates strongly with the research reported by Stronge (2002) and McEwan (2002), the ideas of Aristotle, and with the common sense advanced by the two mothers in the prologue. Michelle and Janice believe that Jenni McLean is an effective teacher and they have an explanation for their judgment. Jenni is working hard to become aware of her students' abilities, needs, and interests, and she knows that she is responsible for providing the instructional leadership so that her students will learn what she teaches them. Jenni's ambitions and practices are strikingly consistent with both common sense and contemporary research findings on what makes an effective teacher.

SHOULD THE MOST EFFECTIVE TEACHERS BE REWARDED?

Since the important characteristics and specifically the strategies that effective teachers use have been identified, would it make sense for the educational system to reward those who are outstanding in promoting students' learning? And what about teachers who are less than effective? Of course, if poor teachers fail to show sufficient improvement within a reasonable time of close supervision and support, then such teachers ought to be dismissed. We doubt that most parents, even most teachers and principals, would disagree with this idea.

However, the reality is that most school districts do not distinguish between effective and ineffective teachers in compensation. Although there are a few notable exceptions, the vast majority of school districts in North America compensate teachers on the basis of two factors, their years of university education and their years of teaching experience. However, these factors have been shown to have very small positive effects on the academic achievement of students, as can be seen, for example, in the research by Eric Hanushek (1986) and Dan Goldhaber (2002).

Building on such findings, Steve Malanga (2001), a senior fellow at the Manhattan Institute, advocates the adoption of a strategy developed by William Sanders at the University of Tennessee, not only to identify the teachers that are more effective in promoting academic achievement but also in compensating their meritorious performance. Sanders's scheme, known as the Tennessee Value-Added Assessment System, has been quite successful in identifying effective teachers and schools that demonstrably improve the performances of their students. As Sanders notes, when variables such as socioeconomic status and family income are controlled, differences in the instructional practices of teachers are, by far, the most powerful factor in explaining the achievement gains of students.

Similar assessment systems are being developed in a number of other states, including Arizona, Arkansas, Florida, Iowa, and North Carolina. As yet, there is very little interest in developing such systems in Canada. Of course, we recognize that there are considerable challenges in implementing any form of merit pay because education is about more than students' academic achievement, and the success of students in schools cannot be attributed easily to one teacher. Consequently, the development of a fair system of evaluating teachers' effectiveness, in all its dimensions, will necessarily involve complexity and controversy.

RECOMMENDATIONS

Many parents become familiar with the teachers and principals in their children's schools. For this reason, they often know who the effective teachers are, and sometimes it is possible for them to enroll their children in classrooms with the most effective teachers. Not surprisingly, teachers and principals are often more understanding and sympathetic to the requests of parents who are involved in the schools. So, we advise parents to get to know the teachers and administrators in their children's schools.

Parents whose children are assigned to an ineffective teacher may need to consider more drastic action. The provisions of some collective agreements, signed by teachers' unions and school districts, have made it difficult for school administrators to discipline underperforming teachers, as illustrated by Scott Reed (2005) and Steven Brill (2009). Nor do all school districts have a managerial culture and specific policies that support the regular review of teachers' performance. Consequently, some senior administrators resort to transferring ineffective teachers to other schools rather than requiring them to improve, or dismissing them if timely improvement is not shown.

In such situations, parents need to courageously present their concerns to the school board. Of course, school boards must act judiciously in the face of complaints and concerns; however, delayed action by a school principal, or the transfer of a teacher whose competence is suspect, helps neither the students currently in the ineffective teacher's classroom nor the students in the school to which the teacher is transferred. If parents are not pleased with the progress shown by the local school authorities, then they will need to take their concerns to the state or provincial level, or send their children to other schools, or educate them at home.

Finally, we think that school districts need to maintain a systematic scheme of teaching assessment and some form of performance-based merit awards for outstanding teachers. Since student learning is the most important goal of education, it is sensible to recognize and reward the most effective teachers who demonstrably improve the performance of students.

School districts should actively promote teaching effectiveness through well-conceived professional development and mentoring programs. Strong support needs to be given to teachers who are already outstanding so that they can mentor other teachers, especially inexperienced beginning teachers. Is the recognition of excellence in teaching not important? At least, such an initiative would stimulate a much-needed public discussion about effective teaching and effective schools.

BIBLIOGRAPHY

Bredemeier, Mary E., and Harry C. Bredemeier. 1978. *Social forces in education.* Sherman Oaks, CA: Alfred Publishing.
This classic text in the sociology of education weds theory with the reality of teachers and students working in effective classrooms and schools.

Brill, Steven. 2009. The rubber room: The battle over New York City's worst teachers. *New Yorker.* August 31.
This article illustrates the difficulties that school administrators have in firing incompetent teachers in New York City.

Clifton, Rodney A., and Lance W. Roberts. 1993. *Authority in classrooms.* Scarborough, ON: Prentice Hall.
This book identifies the basic characteristics of effective teachers and effective schools.

Evers, Williamson M., and Lance T. Izumi, ed. 2002. *Teacher quality.* Stanford, CA: Hoover Institution.
This book examines the empirical literature on the most effective teaching practices.

Goldhaber, Dan. 2002. The mystery of good teaching: Surveying the evidence on student achievement and teachers' characteristics. *Education Next* 2 (1).
This article is a good survey of the research literature on teachers' effectiveness, pointing out that verbal ability, subject-matter knowledge, and experience within the first five years have significant effects on their students' academic achievement. Surprisingly, teachers' college education, teachers' degrees, and more than five years of experience have virtually no effect on their students' academic achievement.

Hanushek, Eric. 1986. The economics of schooling: Production and efficiency in public schools. *Journal of Economic Literature* 24 (3): 1141–77.
This research examines the effect that years of university and years of teaching experience of teachers have on their students' academic performance.

Surprisingly, it finds that there is little, if any, relationship between these two factors and the academic achievement of students.

Hare, William. 1993. *What makes a good teacher.* London, ON: Althouse Press. This is a philosophical examination of the virtues and intellectual qualities of effective teachers.

Lortie, Dan C. 1977. *School-teacher: A sociological study.* Chicago: University of Chicago Press. This classic in the sociology of teaching portrays the experiences of public school teachers in North America.

Malanga, Steve. 2001. Why merit pay will improve teaching. *City Journal* 11 (3). A senior fellow at the Manhattan Institute highlights the research of William Sanders and his value-added assessment system as an example of how to assess the performances of teachers and how to reward those who are most effective.

McEwan, Elaine K. 2002. *Ten traits of highly effective teachers: How to hire, coach, and mentor successful teachers.* Thousand Oaks, CA: Corwin Press. This book discusses the most important traits of effective teachers and explains how administrators can hire, mentor, and coach them.

Raham, Heather, Neil Guppy, Susan M. Phillips, and Kristen Bennett. 2008. *Beyond the grid: A Canadian look at the terrain of teacher compensation.* Kelowna, BC: Society for the Advancement of Excellence in Education. This Canadian report examines several school districts in the United States that have incorporated various forms of merit pay into their compensation schemes for teachers.

Reed, Scott. 2005. *The hidden costs of tenure.* Springfield, IL: The Small Newspaper Group. http://thehiddencostsoftenure.com. A series of newspaper articles on the teacher tenure system in the state of Illinois, conducted over a six-month period, shows that the tenure system makes it almost impossible for school administrators to fire incompetent teachers.

Stronge, James H. 2002. *Qualities of effective teachers.* Alexandria, VA: Association for Supervision and Curriculum Development. This monograph summarizes the empirical literature on effective teachers. The research findings and the comprehensive assessment instrument are useful for teacher educators, beginning and experienced teachers, and parents who are interested in the effectiveness of teachers.

6

Some Schools Are Better Than Others

PROLOGUE

Marcus and Harriet Scott were sitting at the kitchen table on Friday night having a frank discussion about their daughter's school. Jeanine was in Grade 4 at Happy Valley Elementary School, and her parents were frustrated with the lax discipline and low academic standards that they saw at the school.

"Several days ago, I phoned Jeanine's teacher to ask if there was anything we could do at home to help Jeanine improve her spelling," began Marcus. "Miss Carver told me that she doesn't believe in correcting spelling because it discourages creativity among her students. How can any teacher actually believe that spelling isn't important?"

"Never mind that," replied Harriet, "earlier today, when I stopped by Jeanine's classroom to drop off her lunch, I couldn't believe the chaos in the classroom. It looks like the teacher doesn't have any control over her students. Several children were running around the classroom, and the teacher was just sitting at her desk reading a newspaper."

As their conversation continued, Marcus and Harriet listed some other things about the school that concerned them—confusing homework assignments that had little to do with practicing basic skills, and the unwillingness of the school's principal to take any of their concerns seriously. All of these things convinced Marcus and Harriet that their daughter was not receiving a good education at Happy Valley Elementary School.

"So what are we going to do about this situation?" asked Harriet. "Can we find a different school for Jeanine? I know there is a private school not too far from us, and it has a very good reputation."

"Well, you know we don't have the money to send her to a private school," said Marcus, with some exasperation. "I wish we did; then we'd be able to get Jeanine out of that terrible school. She needs a good education to make a living in this world—that's my worry."

Harriet thought of another option. "What about seeing if we can send Jeanine to another public school in the district? I hear from friends at work that Greenfield Elementary is a good school. Several of my friends have their kids enrolled there, and from what I hear, they are receiving a much better education than our daughter. Since Greenfield is right by my workplace, I'd even be able to drop off Jeanine at the beginning of the day and pick her up shortly after school is finished in the afternoon."

Marcus shook his head. "I already checked out that possibility by phoning the school district office. It turns out that they have a policy that really discourages enrolling students in schools outside their neighborhood catchment area. So, the only way we can guarantee that Jeanine gets into Greenfield is to move to that neighborhood."

"But we can't afford to move there!" exploded Harriet. "The houses are much too expensive for us. We'd never be able to afford the mortgage payments, never mind the property taxes. Why won't the school district let us choose the school that we want? It's not like the schools are overcrowded."

"I didn't understand it myself when they explained it to me," replied Marcus. "They said it was about maintaining the integrity of the neighborhood school community or something like that."

"Well, that means our daughter will not be well educated. It's time that we put some pressure on the school board to change that policy," said Harriet defiantly. "We deserve to have a say in where our daughter goes to school and we want her in a better school. She needs to get a good education, and I'm worried about her future, too."

INTRODUCTION

Marcus and Harriet are feeling powerless because their daughter is required to attend a school that they think is unsatisfactory. Sadly, there is little these parents can do about it. The principal of Jeanine's school is unwilling to address their concerns, and the school district effectively restrains them from registering Jeanine at another district school. Her parents don't have enough money to send her to a private school, they can't home school her, and they don't have the money to buy a house in a neighborhood close to a better public school. All things considered, it looks as though the Scott family had better make the best of Jeanine's time at Happy Valley Elementary School because she will be going there for at least two more years.

Unfortunately, across North America, thousands of families find themselves in similar situations. Trapped in unsatisfactory schools, many children from low- and moderate-income families receive a substandard education in comparison with children from upper-income families who live in, or can move to, neighborhoods with better public schools, or who can afford to send their children to private schools.

Although some educators claim that one school is as good as any other, that all schools are equally good, just different, or that such judgments cannot be made fairly, most parents, teachers, and principals know this is not true. The research literature is absolutely clear: some schools are better than others and, in fact, researchers have identified the characteristics of the most effective schools.

WHAT MAKES SCHOOLS EFFECTIVE?

In his important book, *What Works in Schools: Translating Research into Action*, Robert J. Marzano (2003) shows that North American public educators, if they properly interpret the wealth of reputable educational research, can meet the challenge of creating and sustaining effective schools: "the research on the effectiveness of schools considered as a whole, paints a very positive image of their impact on student achievement [and] the schools that are highly effective produce results that almost entirely overcome the effects of student background" (6–7). There is a very good chance that all schools can become more effective, he argues, if educational policy makers accept the "consistent conclusion in the research literature," that "the school (as opposed to the district) is the proper focus for reform" (10), and the policy implication that "school choice" must be seen as a most "viable way to implement the findings from the research" (9).

Marzano's (2003) synthesis of the research literature on school effectiveness is a comprehensive and compelling categorization of school-level factors

that have been shown to influence students' academic achievement. He identifies these factors as chiefly a function of school-wide policies and initiatives
that are monitored and sustained by an assertive school administrator who is
a guiding and cohesive force. Specifically, he identifies six characteristics of
effective schools; namely, strong school leadership, a safe and orderly school
environment, a guaranteed and viable curriculum, challenging academic
goals and effective feedback, professional and collegial teachers, and parental
involvement and community support. In his view, these factors can be addressed without any major addition of school resources.

1. Strong School Leadership

This factor is pervasive and influences all of the others. An effective school
has an effective leader, and it is easy to see why. The principal's role is rightly
seen as crucial, but not alone crucial; the teachers are crucial, too, because
they are closest to the intersection of teaching and learning. Effective schools
have effective teachers who can follow capable leaders because they point
the way to improved academic success. It is ideal if the principal is seen as
the leading professional, the "titular and conceptual leader" (Marzano 2003,
174), who can keep everyone focused on the important work of the school.

Administrative leadership affects every teacher-level factor (for example, the
teachers' classroom management strategies that support the students' learning)
and every student-level factor (for example, the student's motivation to learn).
The teacher-level factors that affect student achievement were the subject of
chapter 5, and the key question there was "what makes teachers effective?"
Here, the key question is a parallel one: "what makes schools effective?"

2. Safe and Orderly School Environment

The importance of this factor for effective schools should be obvious. There
is considerable evidence to show that students need, and parents expect, safe
and orderly schools. Any violence in schools is worrisome to everyone, and "a
school that does not attend to this factor risks undermining all other efforts
at school improvement" (Marzano 2003, 54). This characteristic rests on the
commonsense realization that a safe and orderly school environment provides the necessary freedom and comfort for teachers and students to pursue
teaching and learning without distraction.

The school policies and disciplinary practices that are designed to secure a safe and orderly school environment were discussed in chapter 3: establish clear, school-wide rules for conduct and interaction that invoke high ethical standards; teach and reinforce the rules by having appropriate consequences for violations of them; identify students who are violent or show extreme behaviors and protect other students and teachers from them; and encourage self-discipline and responsibility as an integral part of the school's program.

3. A Guaranteed and Viable Curriculum

A guaranteed curriculum means that the knowledge and skills to be learned by the students are specified by the state or province, the school district, and the school. For the curriculum to be viable, the curriculum content must be adequately addressed in the instructional time actually available to teachers. The significant practical implication of this requirement is that teachers must teach the mandated curriculum; they do not have the discretion to ignore or replace it.

Assertive school leadership by the principal, and the dedication of the teachers, is required because the essential knowledge and skills must be clearly communicated to the students and their parents, it must be actually taught in the classroom, and the instructional time available must be protected and used wisely. Specifically, the content of the curriculum must be orchestrated by the teachers so that the students have an ample opportunity to learn it.

The opportunity to learn (OTL), a concept in use for over four decades in the research literature, is a measure of the extent to which the mandated *intended curriculum* is equivalent to the *implemented curriculum* of the teacher and the *attained curriculum* actually learned by the students. The notion of OTL as an aspect of effective schools is, as Marzano (2003, 24) observes, "a simple but powerful one—if students do not have the opportunity to learn the content expected of them, there is little chance that they will."

Because curricular mandates are ultimately the responsibility of states or provinces, these authorities have an important regulatory role for ensuring that instruction time in schools is sufficient to allow the mandated curriculum to be implemented and attained. The principal must ensure that the mandated curriculum is actually taught to the students.

4. Challenging Academic Goals and Effective Feedback

This factor of school effectiveness is a combination of high but reasonable expectations and requirements for student success, and appropriate and frequent monitoring of student progress. Establishing academic goals has a distinct advantage, both for school-wide targets (for example, improving the percentage of students in the school who are at or above grade level in reading) and specific individual student goals. It says that achievement is important for all students, particularly for students from low socioeconomic backgrounds, "a cornerstone of the school effectiveness research" (Marzano 2003, 36). Indeed, the recognition of this fact is likely very important for schools whose student populations have a significant representation of ethnic and cultural minorities—notably, blacks and Latinos in the United States and Aboriginal students in Canada—because of the considerable overlap, evident in the research literature, between the students' socioeconomic status and their ethnicity or minority cultural group membership.

Then, there is this question: how will the school and teachers know if the academic goals are being met? Setting goals is only the first step—it must be followed by, and carefully aligned with, a rigorous monitoring, assessment, feedback, and reporting scheme. Feedback must meet specific requirements: it must be specific to the knowledge and skills to be learned and the targets set; timely and available at multiple, predictable times throughout the year; and strongly based on formative classroom assessments, except for end-of-year summative assessments that may be standardized.

Significantly, Marzano (2003) provides a detailed illustration of such a scheme. It is based on quarterly assessments—every ten weeks in a school year of forty weeks or two hundred days, and includes a sample report card that represents individual student achievement by letter grades, based on a percentage scale, for every subject and for the major knowledge topics and academic skills in each subject, together with a sample teacher grade book and a model of performance standards for the guaranteed curriculum. His message is crystal clear: securing the efficacy of this requirement for effective schools requires detailed planning and careful measurement of progress on the academic goals.

5. Professional and Collegial Teachers

This factor focuses on the way teachers perform their work and interact with each other, as well as with students, administrators, and parents. In effective schools, respect, courtesy, cooperation, and supportive behavior are prized, yet professional norms and the expectations of teachers enable "openly sharing failures and mistakes . . . and constructively analyzing and criticizing practices and procedures" (Marzano 2003, 61). Notably, this description of professional and collegial relations is a departure from the usual one that tends to interpret collegiality as involving primarily relationships of friendship. In professional encounters, where the considered judgments of colleagues may sometimes result in strong disagreements, congeniality is not mistaken for collegiality.

A significant feature of professionalism is the teachers' sense of efficacy, that is, the belief that they can change the classroom and the school for the better, and that their pedagogical knowledge, subject-matter knowledge, and experience is a strong basis for participation in school-wide decisions. The good administrator strongly supports this participation. The wise administrator also knows that this expectation extends to the nature, scope, and sequence of teachers' professional development.

Marzano (2003), in fact, provides a somewhat pessimistic assessment of much professional development in schools: it reveals a view of teachers and their development that too often fails to engage the intellectual struggle inherent in teaching in ways that "deepen the discussion, open up the debates, and enrich the array of possibilities for action" (66). In effective schools, those professional development activities showing the strongest relationship to teacher behavior that improves academic achievement are used. These activities emphasize content and pedagogical knowledge; the teachers' examination of the various strategies as to their effect on achievement in their classrooms; and one session builds on another so that the program is coherent.

6. Parental Involvement and Community Support

Parental involvement is shown to be an aspect of effective schools, and community involvement, less explicitly so. The defining feature of this aspect of effectiveness at the school level is the existence of specific mechanisms for communication, participation, and consultation. Good communication from the school to parents, and vice versa, is a mark of effectiveness, though the most routine and formal communications used by schools are report cards, newsletters, and bulletins, which usually provide only a limited opportunity for parental responses.

Of course, schools have the greater responsibility for initiating communi-cation and inviting participation, and this is most successful where the school welcomes parents and community members, some of whom offer valuable expertise and resources. Providing explicitly for consultation with parents on matters that relate most directly to the achievement of their children and the quality of their school experience is only reasonable, indeed is common sense—people who are affected by decisions that concern their children's education should be involved in making them. Because of their involvement, parents are likely to be more informed about, and accepting of, the decisions made. However, serious criticism by parents and conflict between parents and school personnel have negative effects.

Legislative requirements for parent-school advisory councils in a num-ber of states and Canadian provinces show that consultation with parents is widely favored. However, there are some fundamental controversies in con-sulting parents that remain unresolved in many jurisdictions. Will parents have a say in the hiring and firing of teachers and administrators? Will schools make available the information that permits parents to know precisely how academically successful their students are?

On the first question there is considerable evidence that parents have little interest in hiring and firing decisions; however, on the second question, the ad-vocates of school choice, a strong and growing movement in both Canada and the United States, contend that the availability of reliable information about the academic success of individual schools is an essential requirement if parents are to be empowered, and schools are to be accountable to the public.

USING SCHOOL CHOICE TO EMPOWER PARENTS

William Ouchi's (2003) study of over two hundred public schools in both Canada and the United States, *Making Schools Work: A Revolutionary Plan to Get Your Children the Education They Need*, clearly shows that the most successful schools have the most decentralized management by principals who are responsible for the hiring of teachers and have primary control of the school's budget, and where parents can choose the schools their children attend. In contrast, school districts that permit little autonomy for princi-pals and allow little parental choice are less likely to improve their students' academic achievement. From the viewpoint of common sense, this suggests that just as competition between sports teams spurs them to higher levels of achievement, schools that compete for students in fair competition will seek to improve their students' academic achievement.

One of the most successful examples of Ouchi's revolutionary plan is the scheme implemented by the Edmonton Public School District in Alberta. Over the last two decades, the superintendent and the school board have allowed the principals to make key managerial decisions and have allowed parents to enroll their children in any of the district schools. Furthermore, schools are held accountable for the achievement of their students through the publication of both school programs and the schools' standardized test results. Consequently, the schools in the district have narrowed their focus to a few attainable objectives. As such, a variety of specialty schools, such as traditional, athletic, and religious, operate within Edmonton's public educational system and parents can choose the school and program that best accommodates the interests and needs of their children.

Because the programs and achievement scores for all schools are published, parents have significant information for making informed choices. Not surprisingly, allowing parents and their children to have these choices, and making reliable achievement data publicly available, has served as a powerful incentive for principals and teachers to ensure that student achievement remains the primary focus while they maintain the special identity of their schools. It is not difficult to see how the lives of Marcus, Harriet, and Jeanine Scott would be different if they were living in the Edmonton Public School District. In short, the Scotts would have a genuine choice of a better school for their daughter.

RECOMMENDATIONS

Unfortunately, not many school jurisdictions in North America provide the degree of choice and school accountability that Ouchi (2003) recommends. Until this situation changes in many more districts, parents, like Marcus and Harriet Scott, will continue to be stymied by educational bureaucracies that are more interested in preserving the status quo than adopting policies and administrative arrangements that improve the academic performance of schools. Obviously, we think that more school boards should implement Ouchi's recommendations. In fact, we believe that all parents, regardless of family income and background, should have the right to select the appropriate school for their children.

The reluctance or refusal of school boards to allow parents to choose schools for their children is especially unfair for low-income families who have limited resources to ensure that their children receive a good education. Of course, to select the appropriate school, parents will need suitable and trustworthy information. Far from weakening the public education system, giving parents more choice would invigorate public education because it would identify and strengthen schools that are successful and provide incentives for less effective schools to improve. We recognize, however, that in rural school jurisdictions there are significant practical limitations to school choice.

The accountability of schools is not as precisely determined as it is in other enterprises or professions where success can be measured in terms of cost and customer satisfaction, and where dissatisfied customers can go to alternative providers. For reasons we set out earlier, parent involvement in schools is strongly justified, and in some jurisdictions there is the recognition that substantial parent involvement may have specific advantages for school governance.

Sometimes, policies imposed by school boards, their superintendents, and provincial or state departments of education engender less commitment than those established by the people who are directly involved in the school. We notice that this tendency has been anticipated and countered in the organization and management of charter schools in some American states and in Alberta, Canada. In these charter schools, substantial parent involvement in local governance has been a distinctive aspect of their success. Is there a lesson in the experience of such schools for school boards and state or provincial authorities? We think so.

Where school choice is not policy, a rigorous scheme of assessment and reporting of students' achievement, including the use of standardized tests, nevertheless can play a key role in strengthening the school's effectiveness and accountability. As such, we recommend that all schools develop a comprehensive system for monitoring students' achievement and progress toward the realization of school-wide goals. Certainly, the school district should give major support to this endeavor, if not specific leadership.

There is little use in schools setting academic goals or having school plans without examining how well the students and the school actually are doing in relation to them. How else can schools be precise and systematic in adjusting

curricular emphases, pedagogical strategies, and school policies if they do not
have the information that enables them to make sensitive and realistic responses to what the evidence on achievement shows? In the absence of goals,
standards of performance, benchmarks of success, and a systematic assembly
of relevant evidence, who is to say what improvement strategies or corrective
action, if any, is warranted in schools to make them more effective?

Consequently, we urge school boards and senior administrators to ensure that they and their principals have an explicit managerial perspective
on effective schools. According to Elaine McEwan (2003), it is essential that
school administrators be "results-oriented," because it is one of the most important characteristics of effective principals, identified in her revealing and
practical book, *Ten Traits of Highly Effective Principals: From Good to Great
Performance.* McEwen (2003) emphasizes that results-oriented principals
"believe that achievement is the bottom line" (124); "never mistake activity
for achievement" (125); "make research-based decisions" driven by data, and
"let the data do the talking" (127); "hold teachers accountable"; and recognize that "if productivity is to be integrated into the organizational culture,
a vehicle for monitoring progress, providing feedback, setting quantifiable
objectives and evaluating performance is a *sine qua non*" (126).

Here McEwan's (2003) highly effective school principal is a mirror image
of Marzano's (2003) strong school leader, suggesting that it is not necessary
for school boards and educational administrators to reinvent the wheel of
school effectiveness. We acknowledge that most educational innovations usually require some tuning to local circumstances, but surely Robert Marzano
(2003), Elaine McEwan (2003), and William Ouchi (2003) provide sufficiently
practical, even exemplary, direction and prescriptions. Can their analysis and
advice readily be adopted by, or adapted easily to, most school jurisdictions?
We think so; all that is required is a familiarity with their works, an appreciation of the rationale for their ideas, and the willingness to implement them.

Many educators, parents, school board members, and members of the
general public say that it is almost impossible to find good schools that do
not have effective principals. This is very likely because effective principals
know, by experience, study, and professional discernment, the distinguishing
features of effective schools and give force and effect to them in their daily
administration. For example, every day, every week, effective principals are
visible throughout the school, in and out of classrooms, walking down the

halls, patrolling the playgrounds, talking to students and teachers, correcting student behavior, and, in general, seeing that the quality of the schooling experience is positive for students and teachers.

In addition to maintaining a safe, orderly, and supportive school environment, they focus on what they know to be their other critical duties—promoting high academic achievement, ensuring a viable curriculum, monitoring academic progress and school improvement targets, hiring effective teachers, and involving parents and community members in the school. Unfortunately, in many schools these primary goals are often ignored or denigrated because peripheral or trivial issues capture too much of the attention of administrators. Thus, we urge all educational administrators to be very discerning and to limit their focus to ensure that their leadership and specific interventions promote effective schools. When bureaucratic requirements or intransigence threaten the achievement of these primary goals, as they sometimes do, effective principals find ways to overcome these obstacles and keep the focus of teachers and students on teaching and learning.

Of course, it is easiest for school administrators to accomplish their primary objectives if they have significant decision-making authority, particularly in relation to the recruitment of the teachers and the administration of their school's budget. This makes it possible for principals to carefully align their resources with the school's educational objectives and to enact changes that are timely and necessary, as Ouchi's (2003) study shows. Also, because principals obviously perform an essential managerial, supervisory, and appraisal role in schools, we think it best that principals not be members of the collective bargaining unit, or union, for teachers.

There is arguably a fundamental conflict of interest if principals belong to the teachers' unions because they are not merely colleagues, they are also agents of the school board with specific duties and authority. Some argue that there is no substantial risk to effective school-level governance where principals are fellow union members with the teachers, as long as principals are thoroughly cognizant of their broad managerial role and are given clear support for it by senior administrators.

We are not persuaded to this view, but we think this argument underscores the necessity for principals to have the confidence and the support of the school board and senior administrators to make the necessary, perhaps even controversial, decisions in the interests of operating their schools effectively.

To avoid any ambiguity that might arise from such circumstances, a few Canadian provinces have, by law, removed school-level administrators from the bargaining unit for teachers.

School boards and their senior administrators must make certain that their school leaders are up to the challenging task of creating and sustaining effective schools, and that no child is ever trapped in an ineffective school, such as the one which Jeanine Scott's parents found so disappointing. Certainly, the selection of effective school leaders is one of the most important decisions that a school board and its superintendent makes. Therefore, just as school districts must have strong programs of professional development for teachers, programs for the recruitment, training, and mentoring of administrators must be equally strong.

We urge school boards to invest in the talents and skills of current and future school administrators who show the most success, dedication, and career promise. In addition, we urge them to broaden their impact in the school jurisdiction by sending principals elsewhere to learn from others' successes in improving schools. In any effort to maximize the benefit of such initiatives, imaginative exchanges or partnerships that place already effective administrators in new environments and circumstances, even outside the school district, can have the broadened impact that school boards need. Certainly, it will take dedicated monies and imagination to achieve these results.

Finally, we encourage parents to raise their concerns with the teachers and the principal of their child's school, and if necessary, with the school board when they think there is a case for district-wide improvements, or even with the state and provincial educational authorities to press concerns that require legislative initiatives. But, even in districts clearly dedicated to the improvement of schools, getting the appropriate changes may be slower and more tedious than some parents, or even teachers, can tolerate while remaining patient.

Those who desire improvement must give principals, teachers, and other officials sufficient time to make the necessary changes. Obviously this will be difficult for parents who are frustrated and believe a school is not serving the educational needs of their children. However, all who have a stake in effective schools—state and provincial governments, school board members, superintendents, principals, teachers, parents, and even students—must work together to help students get the education they deserve.

BIBLIOGRAPHY

Bennett, William J., Chester E. Finn Jr., and John T. E. Cribb Jr. 1999. *The educated child: A parent's guide from preschool through eighth grade.* New York: The Free Press.
This is an extremely important book by three well-known educators who outline the expectations that parents should have for teachers, school principals, and senior administrators in school districts.

Good, Thomas, and Jere Brophy. 1986. School effects. In *Handbook of research on teaching,* ed. Merlin C. Wittrock, 570–602. New York: Macmillan.
This is a classic chapter summarizing the characteristics of effective schools and noting, not surprisingly, that principals are extremely important in organizing and managing effective schools.

Lortie, Dan C. 2009. *School principal: Managing in public.* Chicago: University of Chicago Press.
This book provides an intensive examination of the daily work of public school principals in the United States. Lortie shows how important these principals are in creating effective schools.

Martz, Larry. 1992. *Making schools better: How parents and teachers across the country are taking action—and how you can, too.* New York: Times Books.
Larry Martz, an editor at *Newsweek,* shows that there are many ways to make public schools better. Not surprisingly, he found that in effective schools, principals and teachers worked cooperatively to make a difference in the educational lives of students.

Marzano, Robert J. 2003. *What works in schools: Translating research into action.* Alexandria, VA: Association for Supervision and Curriculum Development.
This book summarizes thirty-five years of research on effective schools, identifies their main characteristics, and provides compelling illustrations of the practical strategies that principals and teachers can use to enhance the academic achievement of their students.

McEwan, Elaine K. 2002. *Ten traits of highly effective teachers: How to hire, coach, and mentor successful teachers.* Thousand Oaks, CA: Corwin Press.
This book discusses ten important traits of highly effective teachers and how administrators can recruit and mentor them.

McEwan, Elaine K. 2003. *Ten traits of highly effective principals: From good to great performance.* Thousand Oaks, CA: Corwin Press.
In a very readable style, and with plenty of illustrations from the trenches, this book identifies the most important personal and professional traits of effective principals.

Ouchi, William G. 2003. *Making schools work: A revolutionary plan to get your children the education they need.* New York: Simon & Schuster.
This book shows how effective schools work and identifies the strategies that committed and skillful school administrators use to improve the academic performances of their students. This is a challenging yet practical book with good advice for superintendents, principals, teachers, and parents.

Phillips, Susan, Helen Raham, and Patrick Renihan. 2003. *The role of the school principal: Present status and future challenges in managing effective schools.* Kelowna, BC: Society for the Advancement of Excellence in Education.
This report, published by a small Canadian think tank, summarizes the characteristics of effective principals drawing on the academic research conducted in Australia, Canada, New Zealand, the United Kingdom, and the United States.

Reimer, Laura. 2008. *Leadership and school boards: Guarding the trust.* Lanham, MD: Rowman & Littlefield.
In both Canada and the United States, the administration of schools rests with school boards composed of elected members. This book reviews many practical ways that board members can help superintendents and principals create and manage effective schools.

II

SOME THINGS ARE PRACTICAL

7

Classrooms Should Be Teacher-Centered

PROLOGUE

Frank and Verna Bradley followed their daughter Joanne down the hallway of Greenway Elementary School as she led them to her Grade 3 classroom. They had not met Joanne's teacher before and this was the first parent-teacher interview of the new school year. Joanne's parents were a little nervous. With only ten minutes slotted for the interview, they wanted to make sure they had time to obtain a clear idea of how Joanne's reading and math skills were progressing.

As they walked into Joanne's classroom, they saw that her teacher had not yet arrived. Frank and Verna quickly looked around the room, and noticed that the desks were arranged in clusters with only a few facing the teacher's desk. Also, they noticed a lot of student-made charts, including the code of conduct, covering the classroom walls. What surprised them most was how cluttered and disorganized the room appeared; a variety of papers, pencils, books, and toys were scattered around the room.

"Welcome to our learning community," said Ms. Robinson as she walked into the room. "Joanne has been looking forward to this student-led conference. Let's have a seat and give Joanne the opportunity to show us what she is learning this year." At this, Ms. Robinson motioned to a small low table in the center of the room with four child-sized chairs.

Frank and Verna exchanged perplexed glances. Verna tried to pull her skirt down below her knees as she settled down on the small chair. Obviously, she was uncomfortable sitting on the small chair.

"Joanne," began Ms. Robinson, "why don't you show your mom and dad the learning goals you've selected for this year and where you feel you've made the most progress so far."

In a shaky voice, Joanne began to explain that she was learning how to read more sophisticated stories and write more complex paragraphs, and she opened her portfolio and showed them several short paragraphs she had written. While Frank and Verna listened attentively to their daughter, they were surprised that Ms. Robinson did not say anything but let Joanne do all the talking. Even when Joanne seemed unsure of what to say and looked at Ms. Robinson, Ms. Robinson merely reminded them that it was Joanne's responsibility to report on her learning progress.

Toward the end of the meeting, Frank decided to speak up. "Ms. Robinson, Joanne tells us about school almost every evening at dinner time. Now, we'd like to get your assessment of Joanne's progress. We are concerned that she might be falling behind in reading, writing, and especially math. We would like to know if she is keeping up with the other students. If not, we would like to help her."

"I appreciate your concern, Mr. Bradley," answered Ms. Robinson. "However, this is Joanne's conference and she will let you know about her progress. We don't rank students, so it would not be appropriate to compare your daughter with other students. I know that Joanne is working hard to meet the goals that she has set for herself."

Frank decided that he had had enough. "But you're the teacher, Ms. Robinson! We want to hear what you think of Joanne's progress. Is she about where she should be, based on your reasonable expectations? Are there any areas where she needs to improve? Isn't it your job to tell us how Joanne is doing?"

Ms. Robinson informed Frank and Verna that their ten-minute conference was up, and another child and his parents were waiting at the door. If Frank and Verna wanted to talk about other things they would need to give her a phone call and set up another appointment. They quickly got up, perfunctorily said good-bye, and walked into the hall where they saw Joanne's friend, Pacha, and his parents. Joanne ran over to Pacha and the two kids began talking while Frank and Verna said hello to his parents.

On their way home, Frank and Verna exchanged their impressions of the conference in hushed voices so that Joanne could not hear them. They were disappointed, and they agreed to talk about it later when Joanne was in bed.

Later that evening, Frank and Verna sat at the kitchen table and talked about the conference they had with Joanne and Ms. Robinson. They thought they would ask for another interview with Ms. Robinson alone, and perhaps after that they would make an appointment with the principal. But, they would also begin looking into other schooling options. Even though Joanne had made good friends at school, including Pacha, it was clear that they were not satisfied with the procedures for reporting their child's progress and they were not happy with Ms. Robinson's educational philosophy.

INTRODUCTION

Clearly, Frank and Verna Bradley have good reason to be disappointed with their parent-teacher interview. They were not told what to expect before the conference, and when they arrived they were confused by Ms. Robinson's approach. Ms. Robinson's style of conducting parent conferences worried Frank and Verna because they thought it was the teacher's job to tell parents how well their daughter was learning, especially the basic skills that are taught in the elementary school years. We cannot fault them for bringing these expectations to the interview.

Unfortunately, instead of talking with the teacher about Joanne's progress, they were required to sit through a conference led by their eight-year-old daughter. Like many parents, Frank and Verna believed that within the guidelines set by the school district and the state, classroom teachers are responsible for setting learning goals, deciding on the appropriate teaching methods, and evaluating the students' progress. To Frank and Verna, it seemed reasonable to hear from the teacher about their daughter's progress, especially in reading, writing, and arithmetic—the core subjects—and how they, as parents, could help her learn. It was unfortunate that what they experienced was a student-led conference that raised new and perplexing questions in their minds.

Indeed, after the conference, Frank and Verna had some unanswered questions. Did Ms. Robinson actually set the goals and plan the learning activities that Joanne presented to them? Is it true, as she claimed, that the learning objectives were established entirely by Joanne? Was Joanne really responsible for monitoring her own progress? Does Ms. Robinson really have no information on how Joanne is doing in comparison with the other pupils? Are the goals demanding enough for their daughter? Or, is Ms. Robinson's description simply a poor explanation of what is really happening?

According to Nel Noddings (1998, 115–19), in student-centered learning the teacher is characterized as a facilitator of learning rather than as an instructor. Direct instruction, workbooks, class-based oral reading, and correcting homework are rarely used, and the learning, evaluating, and reporting on what has been learned are largely delegated to the students. It is apparent that Ms. Robinson is a follower of this educational philosophy. Nevertheless, Frank and Verna's questions deserve to be answered.

WHY NOT STUDENT-CENTERED?

Almost thirty years ago, Carl Bereiter and Midian Kurland (1981, 20–21), well-respected educational psychologists, recognized some of the weaknesses in the child-centered approach to teaching that remain valid today. Specifically, they observed that: "Child-centered approaches have evolved sophisticated ways of managing informal educational activities but have remained at a primitive level in the design of means to achieve learning objectives. . . . [The] analysis of learning problems tends to be vague and irrelevant, big on name-dropping and low on incisiveness . . . it does not appear to be an acceptable way of teaching. . . ."

Surely, the idea that students are expected to select the learning goals and to monitor their own progress is a wrongheaded way of teaching students, especially Grade 3 students. Where is the research or the common sense that says this idea works? This is an important question because child-centered learning appears to trivialize the teacher's knowledge, experience, and judgment. Consequently, we are skeptical of learning philosophies and practices that minimize the impact that teachers have on students' learning. We think that teachers have legitimate responsibilities for planning lessons, teaching, and assessing the students' understanding of the curriculum.

Many professors of education recommend that teachers use student-centered approaches to teach and discipline their students (see Kramer 1991). Rather than having teachers inform the students about their expectations, romantic progressive teachers involve them in deciding the classroom rules. Alfie Kohn (2003), a well-known advocate for student-centered learning, says that the main cause of discipline problems in schools is the teachers' desire to remain in control. Instead of controlling students directly, he says that teachers should create democratic communities. Kohn argues this is preferable to simply enforcing rules that teachers and principals have already decided.

But surely it is paramount that classroom rules be decided and enforced by teachers and·principals, often in consultation with parents, if classrooms are to be effectively managed for the education and safety of students. Of course, students must be responsible for making choices, but this does not require a so-called democratic classroom. In fact, the school cannot be a democracy for many reasons; legislation, public policy, mandated curricula, parental expectations, and the legal and professional responsibilities of teachers all point toward the teachers and principals being required to set the rules and ensure that the students learn the subject matter that has been mandated.

Educators who are romantic progressives have, in fact, created a caricature of teacher-centered classrooms when they say that students are merely passive receptacles to be filled with knowledge. These romantics often call workbook exercises "drill and kill," for example. In the minds of these teachers, student-centered classrooms are filled with active and engaged students who eagerly explore complex topics and set challenging learning goals for themselves. In such classrooms, the teacher is considered a fellow learner with the students.

While effective teachers often recognize that they must take the needs and interests of students into consideration, the current emphasis on student-centered instruction and conferences is fundamentally misguided. It is simply not true that students always know what is best for themselves.

Teachers are professionals and, as such, they are responsible for structuring and assessing the students' learning. Nevertheless, effective teachers balance teacher-centered instruction with student-centered learning activities to keep their students learning the appropriate subject matter in interesting and challenging ways. Handing this responsibility over to students and allowing them to set their own goals is an abdication of the legitimate responsibility of teachers and principals. Taken literally, it invites chaos into classrooms and schools.

WHY TEACHERS SHOULD BE BOTH STUDENT- AND TEACHER-CENTERED

For romantic progressives, it is heretical to suggest that schools need more teacher-centered classrooms. Judging by the number of school districts that identify themselves as student-centered in their mission statements, this philosophical approach has become dominant across North America. Even though the idea of student-centered classrooms may be seductive, Bereiter and Kurland (1981) point out that there are a number of very good reasons to believe that this type of learning is misguided.

Imagine observing a Grade 11 chemistry classroom with twenty-five students. It is the first day of school and the teacher walks into the room. Out of the twenty-six people in the room, who would you expect to have the best understanding of chemistry? If you said the teacher, welcome to the world of common sense. Obviously, the chemistry teacher, who has taken university courses in chemistry, has knowledge and understanding that the majority of students, if not all of them, currently lack. That's why the children in school are called students while the teachers are paid for their knowledge and their ability to transmit that knowledge to the students.

In the case of the high school chemistry class, should the teacher be teacher-centered or student-centered? The simple answer is both. It is pedagogically responsible for teachers to attend to the students' understanding, interests, and backgrounds, and then on the basis of their preparation and training, knowledge, and experience, to teach them what the students need to know. But, since the teacher understands chemistry at a much higher level than the students, would we not expect the teacher to be in control and set the agenda for the course? For worthwhile learning to take place, teachers need to spend considerable time deciding how to present certain concepts, ideas, and calculations to the students and showing them how to solve chemistry problems.

Laboratory work in chemistry, obviously, is more student-centered, but this learning activity is designed to reinforce principles and knowledge that the teacher has already taught, or will teach, in other ways. Without proper preparation, direction, and explicit instruction, some lab work will fail to demonstrate the principles or reinforce the knowledge that the teacher intends. Moreover, some chemical experiments are dangerous for students, and for this reason alone, teachers must closely supervise the students while they are doing experiments in a lab.

Obviously, effective teachers use a variety of strategies and techniques to help students learn a subject; some of them will be teacher-centered and some will be student-centered. We think that parents would be concerned if high school chemistry teachers only used student-centered strategies and allowed the students to decide their own learning goals and construct their own understandings of chemistry. Some students could set their goal to learn as much chemistry as possible while others could set their goal to learn as little as possible. Is this choice sensible? Certainly not, and no self-respecting and competent teacher would allow it.

Essentially, this reasoning applies to every subject at every grade level. Most parents expect that teachers have a better understanding of the subject matter than students, and that they have the skills and ability to teach the students. If so, why should students, parents, and taxpayers tolerate having the students determine the learning goals? Teachers are granted authority, and they are paid, because they have the knowledge and skills to teach the students. If teachers are not better versed in the subject than their students, and if they cannot promote greater understanding of the subject matter, then they should not be given authority in classrooms and they should not be paid as teachers.

Let's return to the scenario with Frank and Verna Bradley and the education that their daughter is receiving. Ms. Robinson has created a very student-centered classroom: she arranges the students' desks in clusters; the students are not facing the front of the room; and apparently the students have drafted the classroom code of conduct posted on the bulletin boards. In fact, in this classroom the students focus on what they want, and Ms. Robinson focuses on the perceived "needs" of the eight-year-old children. Does she not have an expert understanding of teaching or the subject matter? Are the students not expected to learn from her? Seriously, does Ms. Robinson want to be seen as just another learner working alongside the third-grade students in a "learning community?"

To us, it seems that this extreme student-centered approach to educating Grade 3 students is either disingenuous or misdirected. All students in every grade need clear directions and instruction from their teachers. By acting like a fellow student rather than a teacher, Ms. Robinson is effectively abdicating her professional responsibility to teach the students what they need to know. Obviously, Grade 3 students need to perfect their reading, writing, and perform more sophisticated arithmetic calculations. Surely, Ms. Robinson, as the teacher, is ultimately responsible for ensuring that the students actually learn these things.

How does teaching and learning take place outside public schools? Once again, the driver education analogy we used before may be helpful. Driver education courses are mainly teacher-centered for a good reason. Can you imagine a driver education academy that called itself student-centered and reduced the responsibilities of instructors to facilitators? What would parents think about a driving instructor saying, "I can't really teach you to drive; you must learn by yourself." Or worse, "You tell me how you want to drive, we will try it out, and then I'll help you drive that way."

In such an academy, the instructors could avoid being "experts." Instead, they would be fellow students who were also learning how to drive. Most people probably recognize the absurdity of allowing student drivers to set their own goals and decide on their own methods of learning to drive. There are already too many traffic accidents without the foolishness of student-centered driving schools.

The answers to the questions posed about Ms. Robinson's classroom role, rhetorical as they are, should be obvious. And the absurdity of a thoroughly student-centered educational philosophy applied to a driving school speaks for itself. Why, then, do we allow this philosophy to dominate many public schools and schools of education?

Obviously, we think that public school teachers are not mere learning facilitators or coaches. In our minds, teachers have the responsibility to ensure that students learn the essentials of reading, writing, poetry, art, music, and all the other subjects that make them educated citizens who will participate effectively in a democratic society. This principle is true for teachers in Grade 3 classrooms as well as for teachers in Grade 12 classrooms. An unhealthy fixation with student-centered education leads to the conclusion that specialized advanced knowledge and training for teachers is unnecessary because teachers are learning alongside their students anyway. Contrary to this romantic view, we argue that teachers must use their specialized education, skills, and the understanding they have of their students to actually teach them and direct their learning in productive ways.

RECOMMENDATIONS

Student-centered education has sometimes been taken to ridiculous extremes. When teachers see themselves as merely learning facilitators or fellow learners with their students, something has gone seriously wrong. Teachers are hired and paid to teach because they have the knowledge, experience, skills, and judgment that the students lack. Let us not lose sight of this fact.

Accordingly, we encourage school boards to examine their policies, starting with their mission statements. While it may make school officials comfortable to say they are student-centered, officials need to carefully consider the problems associated with promoting this romantic philosophy of schooling. Of course, it is important for teachers to be student-centered by taking their students' abilities, needs, and interests into account when they set goals, establish their methods of teaching, and design their evaluation procedures. But in doing this, teachers need not accept an educational philosophy that makes no sense to reasonable parents like Frank and Verna Bradley or to many other parents, teachers, principals, and educational thinkers.

To parents, we recommend carefully examining the philosophy that teachers espouse in their children's classrooms. If your experience is similar to Frank and Verna Bradley's, let your teachers and principals know that you want strong teacher leadership and that you need to know how your children are progressing academically. Don't let teachers and principals speak in generalities about your children's progress or simply assert their adherence to a romantic progressive philosophy of education. Above all, insist on unambiguous answers to your questions about how your children are doing in school. Education is too important to leave the major learning decisions to the children.

We have created public schools and hired well-educated, skilled, and dedicated teachers because we expect them to teach and evaluate students. For this to happen, classrooms must be teacher-led while not forgetting that the subject matter must be challenging and interesting for the students. Effective teachers understand that they need to consider the abilities, needs, and interests of their students, but that they are ultimately responsible for helping them learn what they ought to know.

BIBLIOGRAPHY

Bereiter, Carl, and Midian Kurland. 1981. A constructive look at *Follow Through* results. *Interchange* 12 (1): 1–22.
Bereiter and Kurland question the romantic progressive interpretation of a very important research study, the *Follow Through* study conducted in the United States.

Brandes, Donna, and Paul Ginnis. 1986. *A guide to student-centred learning.* Oxford: Blackwell.
Brandes and Ginnis summarize the arguments for student-centered learning and describe how it can be implemented at all grade levels.

Kohn, Alfie. 2003. Almost there, but not quite. *Educational Leadership* (March): 26–29.
    Kohn argues that public school teachers are not student-centered enough and ought to devolve considerably more authority and responsibilities to students.

Kramer, Rita. 1991. *Ed school follies: The miseducation of America's teachers.* New York: The Free Press.
    Kramer is a well-known journalist who spent a year visiting schools of education throughout the United States. She exposes some of the absurdities that student teachers are taught and provides considerable insight into why so many teachers have bought into the romantic progressive philosophy and student-centered education.

Nikiforuk, Andrew. 1993. *School's out: The catastrophe in public education and what we can do about it.* Toronto: MacFarlane Walter & Ross.
    In this survey of Canadian public education, journalist and former teacher Andrew Nikiforuk provides specific examples of the follies of student-centered education in Canada.

Noddings, Nel. 1998. *Philosophy of education.* Boulder, CO: Westview Press.
    Noddings summarizes a number of philosophical perspectives on education in a primer for people who want a better understanding of the range and depth of thinking about educational aims and methods.

8

Direct Instruction
Is Good Teaching

PROLOGUE

It was Monday morning and Grade 11 student Wilma Li was looking forward to beginning her American history course at Hendrickson High School. Wilma hoped that the new teacher, Mrs. Merrifield, would follow in the footsteps of Mr. Reynolds, a revered history teacher at Hendrickson who had just retired.

Throughout his long career, Mr. Reynolds held his students spellbound with his fascinating lectures and penetrating questions. His reading and writing assignments were particularly challenging because he required his students to do considerable research, and Wilma and her friends had found reading the original documents and different interpretations of them worthwhile in the Grade 10 world history course they had taken with him. Like all the teachers at Hendrickson High, he challenged all students to succeed, and expected almost all of them to attend college.

As Wilma walked into Mrs. Merrifield's classroom, she took a moment to collect her bearings because the desks were arranged in clusters of five throughout the room. A young woman Wilma assumed was Mrs. Merrifield cheerfully greeted her and offered to help her find a desk so she could sit with her friends. After the buzzer sounded and class began, Mrs. Merrifield introduced herself, handed out the course outlines, and began explaining how the course would be taught.

"I know that students don't want to be treated like passive learners," began Mrs. Merrifield, "so you will find that I will do very little direct teaching in this course. In fact, I see myself more as a guide by the side than a sage on the stage. I want each of you to feel included as members of a learning community, of which I, too, am a member."

Wilma wasn't sure what to make of Mrs. Merrifield, and she was puzzled by her introduction. What did she mean that she didn't want to be a "sage on the stage"? And, what exactly was this learning community she was apparently joining? But, there was more.

"Because there is so much of value in this course, I will not be choosing the topics that will be studied," continued Mrs. Merrifield. "Instead, the five students in your cluster will be responsible for forming expert groups that will research topics that interest you and your group will present a report to the other students. Also, I won't be assigning a textbook because I want you to think and conduct research like historians; I want you to find your own resources."

"This sounds a little strange," thought Wilma to herself. "How are we supposed to decide what topics are important? Isn't that the teacher's job? I've never taken a course on American history, and I really don't understand how I'm supposed to think and work like a historian."

The next two weeks of the course confirmed Wilma's worst fears. Her group of five had three of her friends who were good students and wanted to go to college and two other students who cared little about marks and consequently their effort was minimal. Mrs. Merrifield rarely taught anything directly to the students; in fact, she gave the impression that she knew very little about American history. The few times she provided comments were when she was summarizing tidbits of information some students had found on obscure websites.

There seemed to be no rhyme or reason to the course, and at the end of the two weeks Wilma was not certain she was learning anything of value. Mostly she had learned incoherent trivia that other students thought was interesting or relevant.

"I wish Mr. Reynolds was still teaching this course," thought Wilma. "He was old-fashioned, but I would have learned a lot more listening to his lectures and doing his assignments than listening to other students talk about things they find interesting but know little about. Can I drop the course and take it by correspondence instead?" she wondered.

INTRODUCTION

Wilma Li's experience in the Grade 11 American history course has been a disappointment. This is unfortunate because it would be fairly easy to make history interesting to most of the Grade 11 students at Hendrickson, particularly students like Wilma who were bright and inquisitive. Mr. Reynolds clearly had succeeded; in fact, students were so impressed that they gave glowing reviews about his course to younger students. Throughout his teaching career, he had inspired hundreds of students to take history more seriously, and many of them went on to study history in college.

TRADITIONAL AND PROGRESSIVE CLASSROOMS

Mr. Reynolds would seem to have been an excellent teacher. The irony is that he is exactly the type of teacher who, because of his direct instruction methods, would be considered by some educators to be most in need of changing his practices to become more modern, progressive, and less traditional. Why? Because he gave systematic explanations and topical lectures, asked specific historical questions, and had students write research papers using proper grammar and punctuation. Incoming students knew that Mr. Reynolds was a stickler for well-written research papers, but he demonstrated and coached them carefully on the form of good writing and on the content of their historical topics.

Does Mr. Reynolds need to apologize for being old-fashioned? Even though his lectures were very interesting and his questions relevant to understanding modern American history and politics, the fact remains that, according to romantic progressive educators, such teaching turns students into passive learners and for this reason such methods should be abandoned. In contrast, Mrs. Merrifield spends very little time lecturing and prefers having students talk about their historical research because she believes their work shows that they are engaged in their own learning.

Progressive educators favor the open-ended methods used by Mrs. Merrifield and are quite disdainful of structured traditional lessons because they believe these methods fail to engage students as active learners. According to the romantic progressives, students who are taught by the methods favored by Mr. Reynolds start believing that they do not need to think on their own.

Moreover, the desks in Mr. Reynolds's room were almost always arranged in straight rows so that the students faced him at the front of the classroom. While this made it easier for Mr. Reynolds to keep the students' attention, progressive educational theorists discourage this arrangement because the teacher should not be the center of attention, rather the students' learning should be the focus. Mrs. Merrifield, on the other hand, created "expert learning groups" with groups of desks facing each other scattered around the room, which made it very difficult for everyone to look at her when she was speaking.

Finally, Mr. Reynolds expected his students to spend a lot of time reading, answering specific questions about history, and completing written assignments. He did not permit the students to present their material in any form they wished, which was encouraged by Mrs. Merrifield. If an assignment was to write an essay, Mr. Reynolds didn't allow students to create plays or write poetry instead of writing essays, but Mrs. Merrifield allowed students to do a number of different things.

While Mr. Reynolds allowed some choices in selected assignments, he always insisted on high standards of organization and writing. Obviously, we think that teachers should use some of the so-called old-fashioned methods of teaching because they, in fact, promote effective learning; we reject many of the so-called progressive methods because they do not always promote effective learning.

LOOKING AT TRADITIONAL METHODS

There are very good reasons for using some traditional teaching methods when we examine the basic ideas that underpin them. We begin with the practice of direct instruction. Direct instruction or didactics (from the Greek word *didasko*, to teach) is a simple concept. Since the teacher has sophisticated knowledge about a subject that the students generally do not understand, the teacher provides a verbal description or exposition and analysis of the subject in a way that elaborates on the subject matter and supplements the information in textbooks written by experts.

Direct instruction may be entirely one-sided, which is obviously inappropriate, or it may be more engaging if questions, assigned readings that challenge conventional interpretations, debates, visual aids, maps, photos, and videos are used to embellish the teacher's explanations, all in an effort to make the subject more understandable and more interesting to the students. Such aids can accompany the teacher's explanations or they can be provided beforehand or afterward, depending on the teacher's objectives for teaching the curriculum and the teacher's assessment of the capacities, needs, and interests of the students.

Essentially, teachers who use direct instruction assume that students are not experts in understanding and interpreting the course material, and if their misinterpretations are not corrected, then the students will have an inadequate understanding of the subject matter. To become educated, students must sort out the relevant data from the mass of information that is available; obviously, effective teachers can help students sort through the information and interpretations without necessarily imposing on them a singular way of thinking.

Romantic progressive educators, on the other hand, are quite disdainful of formal lectures and they typically characterize didactic or expositional teaching as mere "telling," which they believe turns students into passive learners who simply parrot their teachers' ideas and interpretations. Of course, we are not in favor of passive students who simply listen to their teachers' talk, repeat what they say, or answer simple-minded questions. In our minds, teachers must rely on students thinking seriously about the subject matter so that they can respond to the incisive and penetrating questions asked by their teachers. Moreover, teachers must be able to respond to questions that the students ask.

There is nothing in traditional teaching methods that precludes good questioning and answering, or robust debates. The criticisms that some romantic progressive educators have of traditional teaching methods are obviously exaggerated, often stereotyping traditional methods that have some redeeming strengths.

Teachers like Mr. Reynolds use direct instruction because it is an efficient and effective way of conveying certain kinds of information in a limited amount of time. In Mr. Reynolds's view, there is a considerable amount of history that the students need to understand and there are a limited number of hours in the school year. If the students know very little American history, having expert teachers like Mr. Reynolds give interesting and informative lectures emphasizing key points, asking penetrating questions, and using maps and photographs to illustrate some important ideas, can be an excellent way for them to understand the key events and the most reliable interpretations of historical events and circumstances.

Teachers like Mrs. Merrifield who choose not to use direct instruction have to find other ways of conveying the relevant information to the students. Because of their teaching philosophy, romantic progressives are likely to rely on having students work in "expert groups" to attempt to discover the most important facts and then create relevant interpretations of the subject matter.

This often involves getting groups of students to study different parts of a subject and then reporting their findings and interpretations to the other students. But, because the students are not experts in the subject, they may often misrepresent or misinterpret facts. These student-centered teaching methods may respond to the particular interests of the students, but they cannot guarantee that the students will develop a sufficiently comprehensive grasp of the subject matter. Unfortunately, these teaching and learning practices often do not involve techniques that ensure the correction of the students' misrepresentations or misinterpretations.

It is revealing that virtually all romantic progressive educators use direct instruction methods when they are trying to convince teachers to adopt their child-centered methodologies. For example, Alfie Kohn, one of the strongest critics of direct instruction, gives dozens of lectures every year trying to persuade teachers not to lecture. Why does he not abandon the lecture format when it is apparently so ineffective? The reason is obvious. Kohn only has a short time to convey his ideas and he realizes that the most effective way of doing it is in a formal presentation that he has composed and organized. Is it not somewhat ironic that Kohn condemns lecturing as an outdated teaching method while lecturing to his audiences?

What about the old-fashioned practice of lining desks up in rows so that the students are facing the teacher who is at the front of the classroom? Kohn also dislikes this practice. In fact, he claims that any classroom with desks in rows should make parents worry about the quality of the education their children are receiving. Moreover, he says that the classroom where rows of desks face the teacher encourages students to think that teachers are the only source of information and the only reliable interpreters of the subject matter. In his mind, students in these classrooms become passive rather than active learners.

But, when Kohn talks to groups of teachers, how are they seated? You've probably guessed correctly; the audience is facing him and hardly anyone is sitting in groups talking to each other. The same thing is true at most teachers' in-service sessions where teachers hear the new ideas about modern methods of guiding students' learning. Even when speakers are arguing against the old-fashioned methods, like direct instruction, the audience is almost always sitting in rows facing the speakers who are almost always standing on a stage. Obviously, everyone seems to accept that the speakers have something useful to say and the audience is expected to be quiet and pay attention to them.

We think it is entirely justified that all teachers are entitled to expect the same attentiveness from their students. While it is obvious that the teacher is not the sole source of information, normally the teacher should be the most knowledgeable person about the subject being studied. For this reason, the teacher's explanations and expectations should receive considerably more attention from the students than the explanations and interpretations from other students.

Obviously we think that this is appropriate, but we do not imply that students cannot ask questions, even penetrating ones, or that they have no valuable contributions to make in obtaining a proper understanding of the subject matter. It simply means that teachers must be regarded as experts who are ultimately responsible for instructing and guiding the students through carefully orchestrated lessons.

Although there are times when group seating or other novel arrangements may be appropriate, there are good reasons for teachers to seat their students in rows. The main reason, of course, is that this arrangement helps to keep the students' attention focused on the teacher and on the ideas that are being carefully conveyed, limiting the risk that some students will be distracted by other students. Furthermore, the arrangement of desks in rows helps to reduce inappropriate social interaction among the students. Every experienced teacher knows that when the desks are arranged in groups so that students face each other, the risk of distraction and confusion increases considerably.

Though some romantic progressives will recoil at the suggestion that teachers should reduce the social interaction among students, even they will have to recognize that classrooms are primarily places of learning, and it is only common sense for teachers to focus on the students' learning as paramount and discourage off-task behavior that undermines valuable classroom time.

We have no problem with teachers choosing alternative seating arrangements to fit their methods of instruction, but we reject the idea that arranging desks in rows is, in principle, something to avoid as educationally unwise.

Another practice that is often challenged as old-fashioned, and therefore rejected, is the unwillingness of some teachers to allow students to complete their assignments in a variety of ways. For example, when traditional history teachers require students to write essays on the causes of the American Revolution using proper grammar, punctuation, and style, then that is exactly what the students must do. Even though some students will find writing a research essay difficult, they are not permitted to substitute alternative assignments such as performing dramatized reenactments of the Revolution, or giving speeches about the moral principles guiding the protagonists.

In the prologue, Mr. Reynolds, the traditional teacher, had his students write research papers because he believed that writing them was an important skill for the students to master, and not just for those students who like writing essays. Even though students could choose their topics from a list, all of them would improve their skills and learn more history by writing research essays. While romantic progressive educators argue that students should be given considerable latitude in how they complete their assignments, traditional teachers accept some choice, but they know that giving the students too many choices often means that important skills will be neglected by some students.

Just because some students prefer acting to writing essays doesn't necessarily justify allowing them to do what they want. We think it is questionable for anyone to believe or claim that students acting in a play are acquiring the same skills as students who write carefully crafted research essays. Certainly students who plan on attending college or university will quickly discover how much they missed by not learning how to write essays. Clearly, teachers must be sensitive to both the advantages and limitations of their instructional choices.

The continuing debate that pits the phonics approach against the whole language approach also exemplifies how teachers who use certain methods of teaching children to read are criticized for being old-fashioned. Obviously, reading is a foundational skill that all teachers must teach and all students must master. Yet, many teachers in the early grades adhere to the whole language approach even though the research evidence clearly shows that students who understand phonics are more likely to be successful readers, particularly children who find learning to read a difficult experience (see Chall 1983).

Educators who support the whole language approach argue that reading cannot be decontextualized; students must learn to read by associating words and sentences within the context of the story and the pictures, rather than by sounding out, phonetically, the syllables in the words. When students come across unfamiliar words, they are expected to guess their pronunciations and meanings from the context rather than from sounding out the words. As a consequence, some students never learn the skills of sounding out words because they have never been taught them.

Douglas Chisholm and Edwin Buettner (1995), for example, note that there is substantial research evidence showing that many young students need to learn phonics because it helps them learn to read and write properly. Unfortunately, every year thousands of North American parents have little choice but to pay private tutors to teach their children basic reading, writing, and mathematical skills. As practicing professional teachers, Chisholm and Buettner (1995) are correct to criticize teachers who simply dismiss traditional teaching methods and replace them with so-called progressive methods. Traditional methods, especially direct instruction, should have an important place in modern classrooms.

RECOMMENDATIONS

We commend teachers who courageously and tenaciously continue to use direct teaching and other traditional methods for the sake of their students' learning. For them, it is common sense to retain methods that are most effective for helping their students learn what they are supposed to learn. In addition, we hope that more of these teachers will become role models for beginning teachers. For the discerning and skilled teacher, ideological choices of teaching methods—progressive methods are superior and traditional ones are bad, or indeed, the reverse claim—should not be allowed to overtake the intelligent, hardheaded advice offered by Elaine McEwen (2002, 81): "Highly effective teachers don't teach in just one way—they have a repertoire of instructional techniques, teaching behaviors, and essential skills on which to draw, depending on the needs of their students, the nature of the subject, and the complexity of the learning outcomes."

If teachers choose teaching methods by following McEwen's advice, then we think that learners are very likely to be well served. We believe that good teachers need the freedom to choose their instructional methods, both traditional and progressive, and should not be considered effective or ineffective solely on the basis of their ideological loyalties or dispositions, but, ultimately, on whether or not the methods they use improve their students' achievement.

Also, we appeal to educational administrators to consider carefully the people they invite to deliver professional in-service sessions for their teachers. Too many administrators invite too many progressive educators so that all their teachers hear is that traditional teaching methods are ineffective and progressive methods are superior. At least some balance should be struck in the choice of speakers who present in-service sessions. We think administrators need to show greater respect for their teachers' own capacity to decide on the best way to teach their students.

Finally, professors of education, who are more often advocates of progressive methods, ought to recognize that their teaching can become a form of advocacy that is not always sensitive to the real classroom circumstances that teachers encounter. As such, their advocacy may discourage student teachers from using traditional methods that may be effective in helping students learn. For the reasons we have stated, it is simply wrong to claim that traditional teaching methods that involve direct instruction are bad for students.

BIBLIOGRAPHY

Chall, Jeanne. 1983. *Learning to read: The great debate*. New York: McGraw-Hill.
   This is a classic book that makes a solid, research-based case for incorporating a
   traditional method, namely phonics, in reading instruction.

Chisholm, Douglas P., and Edwin G. Buettner. 1995. Whole language: The dawn of
   the new orality? In *Crosscurrents: Contemporary Canadian educational issues*, ed.
   Lance W. Roberts and Rodney A. Clifton, 150–63. Scarborough, ON: Nelson Canada.
   This excellent article makes a case for adopting the techniques of both phonics
   and whole language for teaching reading.

Holmes, Mark. 1998. *The reformation of Canada's schools: Breaking the barriers to
   parental choice*. Kingston, ON: McGill-Queen's University Press.
   A retired school administrator and professor from the Ontario Institute for
   Studies in Education, University of Toronto, argues against the dominant

romantic progressive mind-set and in favor of more traditional approaches of teaching and managing schools.

Izumi, Lance, and Williamson Evers, eds. 2002. *Teacher quality*. Stanford, CA: Hoover Institution Press.
This collection of articles examines the most effective teaching practices supported by both research evidence and common sense.

Kohn, Alfie. 1999. *The schools our children deserve: Moving beyond traditional classrooms and "tougher" standards*. Boston, MA: Houghton Mifflin.
This book is a one-sided attack on traditional teaching methods and provides wholesale advocacy of romantic progressive methods.

McEwen, Elaine K. 2002. *Ten traits of highly effective teachers: How to hire, coach, and mentor successful teachers*. Thousand Oaks, CA: Corwin Press.
McEwen characterizes effective teachers as virtuosi, and provides a comprehensive discussion of their personal, intellectual, and instructional attributes and skills.

Nikiforuk, Andrew. 1993. *School's out: The catastrophe in public education*. Toronto, ON: MacFarlane Walter & Ross.
A journalist and former teacher examines the Canadian public education system and finds performance standards are seriously lacking. Nikiforuk argues in favor of direct instructional methods of teaching and against romantic progressive methods.

Rote Learning and Practice Are Important

PROLOGUE

It was 8:30 p.m. and Grade 5 student Greg Tilson was making very slow progress finishing his math homework.

"Greg, are you still working on your math assignment?" asked his mother, Kathy. "You've been sitting at the kitchen table for over an hour, and you haven't done much."

"This assignment is really hard, Mom," Greg replied. "Some of these math problems are impossible." He pointed at the problem that was currently giving him difficulty: "Keisha has decided to pick one-third of the carrots from her garden. If earlier in the spring she planted 7 rows of carrots, and 24 carrots germinated in each row, how many carrots will be left in the ground after Keisha finishes picking one-third of them?"

Kathy took a quick look at the problem and asked Greg what he should do first. Greg said he wasn't sure, but he thought that it must have something to do with multiplication and division because they had been studying that in school. After Kathy suggested that the first step was to find out the total number of carrots by multiplying seven times twenty-four, Greg reached for the calculator beside his book.

"What are you doing?" asked his mother incredulously. "You don't need a calculator to multiply seven times twenty-four. You can do that on a piece of paper or in your exercise book."

"Mr. Jackson said that we could use calculators any time we need them. He told us that he wants us to focus on a deeper understanding of math and not to get hung up on stuff that a calculator could do," explained Greg.

"Well, in this house we don't use a calculator to figure out something that we can easily do on a piece of paper. Put the calculator away, and write seven under twenty-four and we'll multiply the two numbers," directed Kathy firmly. "Now, what is seven times four?"

"Uh, I dunno," stammered Greg. "We never learned that. We use our calculators all the time."

Kathy couldn't believe what she heard. "Don't you do multiplication drills in school so that you learn this stuff? When I was in school, we had the multiplication tables to twelve times twelve memorized by Grade 5." The blank look on Greg's face confirmed Kathy's worst fears.

"Never mind," sighed Kathy. "Let me help you with the other problems." After thirty more painful minutes of taking Greg through each step in the five math problems, Kathy was just about ready to scream in frustration. Finally, Greg began to see how to tackle the problems, and he came up with the correct answers. "Okay Greg, it looks like we're finally done these four problems. Now put your books away," said Kathy.

"Wait, Mom," interrupted Greg. "I still have to fill out my math journal."

"Your what?" asked Kathy, eyebrows raised.

"My math journal," explained Greg. "Mr. Jackson says that at the end of each assignment we need to write in our math journal and tell him how we feel about math. We're also supposed to come up with suggestions about new ways to solve math problems."

Kathy decided she had heard enough silliness about Mr. Jackson's teaching methods. "We're done for today, Greg. I'll write a note you can take to Mr. Jackson that explains why you couldn't get your math journal finished."

"No, Mom, you can't do that. I'll get into trouble."

"Don't worry, I'll write a nice note so you won't get into trouble," said Kathy to her son. "Now, go to bed; it's late, and I have a university assignment of my own to finish."

When Greg went off to bed, Kathy began thinking about this experience. After weighing various options, she decided to call her son's teacher and find out exactly what was going on in the math course. Then, she would decide what further action was warranted. Whatever happened, she knew that something would have to change in her son's education.

INTRODUCTION

Kathy's frustration is understandable. She has just discovered that her son was unable to perform a simple multiplication exercise despite being in Grade 5. By now, Greg should have mastered the basic procedures for adding, subtracting, multiplying, and dividing, at least for two- and three-digit numbers. As Kathy found out, Greg was unable to multiply seven times twenty-four on a piece of paper, and that made it impossible for him to solve the math problems without the aid of a calculator. Nor did Greg understand the operations that he should do first, next, and last to solve the problems. In light of these difficulties, the teacher's homework assignment seemed pointless.

To make matters worse, had Kathy been working with Greg on his English Language Arts assignments, she would have discovered that his spelling and grammar are just as weak as his math skills. A conversation with the principal would have revealed that Mr. Jackson and all the other teachers at the school favored an inventive spelling and grammar approach in teaching English, which they would say permitted the students to be creative. The principal and teachers do not believe that students should be subjected to spelling dictations, correcting sentence structures, or memorizing spelling and grammar rules. As a result, Greg regularly misspells a number of words and cannot write basic sentences correctly.

What is going on at Greg's school? Simply put, Mr. Jackson and the other teachers are avoiding something that they dismissively refer to as "rote learning and boring practice." With a strong focus on memorization, rote learning is best known for its emphasis on learning by repetition or directed practice. Multiplication drills or "times tables," spelling tests, and memorizing poetry are examples of rote learning that are not favored in Greg's school. Sometimes rote learning and practice is dismissed as "drill and kill." Some teachers, such as Mr. Jackson, claim that rote learning and practice should be shunned because it gets in the way of students' gaining a deep understanding of the subject matter.

Mr. Jackson may be a fictional character but, unfortunately, his teaching methods are used in a number of schools across North America. Teachers who require their students to spell correctly or memorize the multiplication tables are often condemned as old-fashioned for using methods that stifle their creative learning.

Instead of summarily dismissing rote learning and practice, we think that these methods should be rehabilitated because they have proven to be effective ways of learning the basic knowledge and skills that are required for students to engage in higher-level learning. There are, in fact, good reasons for using rote learning and practicing skills in classrooms, and teachers must not be afraid to have their students memorize basic facts and procedures, to recite rules and principles, and to practice necessary skills.

DOES DRILL KILL?

If you ask romantic progressive educators to tell you what they think about rote learning, you will probably hear a long list of the dangers of having students recite "mere facts" about which they have little or no understanding. With such a description, one conjures up images of teachers standing in front of students having them recite, from memory and often in unison, canned responses to predetermined questions.

If these students are asked an original question about what they have learned, or asked a standard question in an original way, you will probably see blank stares in their eyes. In short, the progressive critics argue that while students may have learned the facts and practiced the skills for an upcoming test, they probably do not understand them, and consequently they will probably forget the facts and the skills as soon as the test is over. More important to the progressive critics, these students have probably not learned how the facts and skills relate to the world in which they live.

Perhaps most readers are nodding their heads in agreement. And, we agree that it is important for students to learn subjects at a deeper level than simply memorizing disconnected facts and practicing useless skills. What teachers would willingly subject their students to shallow understanding or memorizing meaningless facts? What parents would agree with teachers who use "drill and kill" methods? Given the choice between meaningful and engaging lessons and mindlessly memorizing facts, virtually everyone would choose meaningful understanding as the proper educational goal. And, so they should.

The main problem with this depiction of rote learning and practice is that it is only half true and does not reflect the real world of learning. To suggest that rote learning automatically precludes deeper understanding is false. Furthermore, critics of rote learning often fail to ask whether the absence of certain kinds of rote learning and well-developed practice exercises makes it impossible to gain a deeper understanding of the subject matter.

To illustrate the importance of these educational strategies, let us examine the way that musicians learn to play their instruments. How do they begin? Do they select an instrument and then immediately begin playing advanced musical compositions? Of course not. To play a musical instrument, students must spend considerable time learning how to hold and play it properly. This is a matter of knowing the proper techniques and practicing them until they become habitual so students can produce a controlled musical sound. There is also the need to identify and use some basic symbols and notations competently.

Students who want to play the flute, for example, will spend hours learning how to hold the instrument, how to blow correctly, and how to move their fingers to obtain the correct notes. Most likely, their music teacher will coach them on the correct techniques. Potential flute players must perfect a considerable number of skills and they must know a number of important things about music before they are able to play complex musical pieces. Most expert players have taken thousands of hours to develop and hone their understanding of music and their performance skills (see Gladwell 2008).

Obviously, to read music, students need to identify the notes that are associated with the various lines on the score, and they need to distinguish between sharps and flats. In addition, they need to know about treble and bass clefs, about whole notes, half notes, and quarter notes, rests, and many other things. In short, potential musicians need to know, by memory, the meanings of many symbols that appear on sheets of music.

They also need to have practiced the skills needed to turn these symbols into pleasing music. Undoubtedly, it takes many hours of memorization and practice to produce the music competently as a composer intended, or if the player is using an improvisational form, to extemporize within the harmonic framework. To play a musical instrument competently requires that students spend many hours practicing and perfecting their skills. Much of this practice, of course, is highly repetitive; some would even say that these practice exercises and rehearsals are boringly repetitive.

Now imagine a music teacher with romantic progressive ideas who argues that all the musical knowledge and skills previously mentioned are inappropriate because they rely on rote learning and boring practice. As a result, this teacher argues that these techniques fail to help students play "real music" because their creativity and originality is inhibited. For this teacher, music students do not need to practice scales or continually repeat songs until they play them correctly.

These students do not need to practice holding their instruments correctly because it is too tedious and too boring, and more importantly, it diminishes their creativity. Furthermore, memorizing all the symbols on the sheet music is not needed because it prevents students from developing a deeper understanding and appreciation of music. Instead, this music teacher would simply urge students to play complex musical scores without burdening them with any rote learning and boring practice sessions.

If you know anything about the rigorous training and sustained practice that professional musicians engage in, your common sense has already recognized that we are being deliberately ridiculous. But, we are simply testing the application of the simple-minded critique of rote learning and practice argued by romantic progressives. Most people probably know that to become competent amateur musicians, students need to practice many, many hours, and they must be able to apply their knowledge to produce a musical result.

In fact, very few people become experts at anything without spending a considerable amount of time learning and practicing, first the basics, and then more advanced skills. As this example illustrates, rote learning and serious practice are not the enemy of deeper understanding and creative expression; rather, rote learning and practice typically provide the foundation for deeper understanding and more creative expression.

We dare to ask: is the acquisition of both knowledge and skills in music, or the skills of competitive sport, all that different from learning to be good at mathematics, science, and language arts? Perhaps it is not too much to suggest that teachers of these subjects could recognize some important things about successful teaching and learning from music teachers and their pedagogical cousins, physical education teachers and coaches. Obviously, we think that drill does not necessarily kill the interest or creativity of students; rather, well-orchestrated drill, the sustained application of basic knowledge and skills, can prepare students for advanced learning.

DOES PRACTICE MAKE PERFECT?

Let's return to the case of Greg Tilson. Greg was unable to complete his math assignment without his mother's assistance for a number of reasons. Fundamentally, he did not know what steps to follow in doing the mathematical operations. In addition, he could not do the simple multiplication without using a calculator. Moreover, Greg could not explain what he should do first, namely, determine the total number of carrots, by multiplication (24 x 7), before calculating, by division, the one-third that Keisha had decided to pick. Consequently, Greg could not calculate the answer, which was the number of carrots remaining in the garden after Keisha picked one-third of them.

Obviously, Greg needs to know more than multiplication to solve this math problem. But, his inability to multiply twenty-four times seven is a serious handicap. Mr. Jackson may think that he is helping Greg by having him use a calculator and not requiring him to memorize the multiplication tables. But, he is actually doing Greg a grave disservice. For Greg, memorizing the times tables means that later on he will not need to struggle with doing simple multiplication without a calculator.

Now, let's turn to Greg's fundamental problem: he could not understand why multiplication was needed or what numbers should be multiplied. Not understanding the procedure to use in answering this problem is a serious obstacle for Greg. What Greg needs to understand is a systematic method of examining the problem to determine the operations he should do first, next, and last to obtain the correct answer. The correct application of basic procedures requires a certain kind of practice; that is, Greg needs to have an overall strategy to follow and he needs several trials and corrections so that he becomes increasingly capable of understanding the problem and then using the correct procedures in obtaining the correct answers.

The form of teaching that describes and illustrates strategies or paths that are reliable in helping students find solutions to problems is called heuristics (from the Greek *heurisko*, to find) by some educators, others call it metacognitive strategies, still others simply call it careful coaching. In fact, Daniel Hallahan and colleagues (2010, 153) say that metacognition "has three components: the ability to (1) recognize task requirements, (2) select and implement appropriate strategies, and (3) monitor and adjust performance." Obviously, Greg needs some metacognitive strategies or some careful coaching.

You might think that Mr. Jackson should have spent more time teaching and coaching Greg and his classmates how to tackle multistep problems systematically. If you think so, you are correct. Both the rote learning of facts and the proper practice of problem-solving strategies are needed to help Greg successfully understand mathematics. Obviously, Greg needs to understand why he is doing the calculations and he needs considerable practice so that he can do them quickly and reliably.

Similarly, practicing spelling and memorizing rules of grammar may not be, in themselves, deep learning, but developing these skills enables students to become more independent learners, and with motivation and practice, can help students become excellent or even creative writers. With the basic understanding and skills mastered, students are prepared to engage in deeper learning; without the basic understanding and skills mastered, students are not prepared to engage in deeper learning.

So, in answering the question, "Does practice make perfect?" we think that successful teachers and coaches know that "Perfect practice makes perfect performance." This answer has a little hyperbole because obviously practicing times tables may help students multiply numbers reliably, but they still may be incapable of solving multistep mathematical problems. Nevertheless, this saying underscores the simple point that practicing skills helps students understand the subject they are studying and this should help them perform better.

When used properly, rote learning and sustained practice can definitely help students develop the foundational knowledge and skills they need to engage in higher-order learning. For these reasons, opponents of rote learning and practice advocate the wrong strategy.

RECOMMENDATIONS

When basic knowledge and skills are not taught and practiced, students will have difficulties in school and in society. Consequently, parents and teachers must make sure that children are taught the fundamental knowledge and skills that are integral to the school curriculum. Where teachers ignore or resist this expectation of parents, like-minded parents must organize and press educators and school board members to ensure that their expectations are met. But, sometimes changing educational emphases takes considerable time and effort. In the meantime, concerned parents may need to send their children to better schools or they may need to hire tutors.

Teachers who think that rote learning and practice is not necessary should reevaluate their reasons for holding this belief. Rote learning and practice make deeper understanding possible for students. Students need to learn important facts and they need to practice fundamental skills. As such, we urge teachers to make sure that their students master the important facts and fundamental skills early in their schooling so that, as they get older, they do not find themselves falling further and further behind their peers. Memorization and practice are important aspects of learning, and their value must not be ignored. Therefore, we urge teachers to give rote learning and guided practice an important place in their lessons.

BIBLIOGRAPHY

Beran, Michael K. 2004. In defense of memorization. *City Journal* 14 (3).
    This article makes a solid case for rote learning and practice in schools.

Butler, D. L. 1998. Metacognition and learning disabilities. In *Learning about learning disabilities*, ed. Bernice Y. L. Wong, 277–307. San Diego, CA: Elsevier Academic Press.
    This chapter identifies the main features of metacognition in the education of disabled students. The principles, however, apply to all students because they are simply the basics of good teaching.

Gladwell, Malcolm. 2008. *Outliers: The story of success.* New York: Little, Brown and Company.
    Gladwell argues that to become skilled at any creative activity takes at least ten thousand hours of dedicated practice.

Hallahan, Daniel P., James M. Kauffman, Laureen J. McIntyre, and David Mykota. 2010. *Exceptional learners: An introduction to special education.* Toronto, ON: Pearson Education.
    This comprehensive book demonstrates that many educational difficulties that students experience require special instructional procedures. The authors explain how these procedures work in real classrooms.

Hirsch, E. D., Jr. 2006. *The knowledge deficit: Closing the shocking education gap for American children.* Boston, MA: Houghton Mifflin.
    This book demonstrates that critical thinking is only possible when students have a solid understanding of the basic knowledge and skills inherent in the curriculum.

Kohn, Alfie. 1999. Getting back to basics. First lesson: Unlearn how we learned. *Washington Post*. October 10.

In this article, Kohn provides a familiar romantic critique of rote learning, practice exercises, and traditional education.

10

A Little Homework Doesn't Hurt

PROLOGUE

Tom Warner was nearing the end of what was turning out to be a very long day. As a first-year Grade 7 teacher at Oak Ridge Middle School, he was wrapping up his second month of teaching. It was a Friday afternoon and his students had just started working on their science assignment, which consisted of reading four pages on electricity in the textbook and answering half a dozen questions in their notebooks. As he walked around the classroom, he could see that over half the students were probably going to finish the assignment before dismissal time.

"Is this assignment going to become homework, Mr. Warner?" asked Jane Randolph, one of his diligent, but slower-working, students.

"Well, there's enough time to get this work finished before you go home so I'll make it due for Monday morning. If you use your time well, it probably won't become homework," replied Mr. Warner.

"No way!" piped up Brad Thompson, a student who frequently made poor use of his time and wasn't anywhere near finishing the work. "My mom said that you're not allowed to give us homework on weekends. It's against the school rules. So you can't make this due for Monday," concluded Brad with more than a trace of smugness in his voice.

With all eyes of the other students on him, Tom realized that he wasn't going to win this battle. "All right," he sighed reluctantly, "the assignment is due on Tuesday morning instead of Monday."

After the students were dismissed, Tom sat at his desk and thought about his exchange with Brad. He decided to look up the official school homework policy to read exactly what it said. After digging through his files, he found a copy of the September newsletter that had a copy of the homework policy on its back page:

> At Oak Ridge Middle School, we value the time children spend with their families, and consequently we minimize the amount of homework each student receives. Total assigned homework shall not take up more than thirty minutes of a student's time on any given evening. In addition, teachers shall not assign homework on the last day of the week or schedule any tests for the first day of the week.

Tom did not see much of a problem with this policy when he first read it in the rush of things he had to do at the end of August and during the first two weeks in September. But now he was beginning to realize how the policy limited his discretion regarding his teaching plans and the timing of assignments.

Because he was not able to tell his students that the science assignment was due on Monday morning, he had little choice but to allow more class time to work on it despite the fact that more than half the students were already finished. Mr. Warner knew that correcting this assignment on Tuesday was going to put his students even further behind schedule because they couldn't go on to the next topic until this one was properly completed. Before proceeding with the science unit, he needed to be sure that the students understood the basic facts about electricity.

Tom Warner pondered his predicament and the school board's homework policy. "The assignment wasn't very long, and the students benefit from the practice questions. What is the big deal about doing a little homework over the weekend? Is it really that harmful?" Though well-intentioned in terms of family time, wasn't the policy simply too restrictive?

Tom shook his head and stood up to leave. "I guess there must be something I'm missing here. The school board wouldn't just make up rules without a good reason, would they?"

INTRODUCTION

While Tom's trust in his school board and senior administrators is admirable, the homework policy he is required to follow may not be. The value of homework in schools has been questioned for a number of years. The critics of homework (see Bennett and Kalish 2006; Kohn 2006) have argued that virtually all homework is pointless busywork that fails to provide any appreciable benefit for students. Because such ideas are increasingly being accepted in many school jurisdictions, along with some parental complaints about the excessive homework requirements of some teachers, it is not surprising that some school boards have enacted policies that place restrictions on the assignment of homework.

For example, in April 2008, the Toronto District School Board in Ontario enacted a homework policy that came about in response to demands from parents and students that the amount of homework assigned was too much. Consequently, a new policy was enacted allowing teachers to assign only minimal homework to elementary students, no more than one hour per evening to Grade 7 and 8 students, and no more than two hours per evening to high school students. Exactly how teachers at large high schools are expected to know how much homework has been assigned by the other teachers is not specified. In addition, the teachers are forbidden to assign homework over holidays, and they are not permitted to discipline students who fail to complete their homework on time.

The Davis Joint Unified School District in California has a policy that goes even further. In addition to restricting the amount of homework that can be assigned to students during the week, teachers are not permitted to give assignments at the end of the week that will be due at the beginning of the next week. Moreover, high school teachers are required to coordinate the amount of homework they assign to ensure that the specified maximums are not exceeded. As expected, the guidelines fill several pages in the district's policy manual. Teachers in that jurisdiction may wonder why they should even bother to assign any homework at all.

We acknowledge that some homework assignments are questionable, especially if they do not relate to curricular objectives and classroom instruction, are too difficult, are often not corrected, or are not returned in a timely fashion. Nevertheless, we ask whether restrictive policies or outright bans on homework are sensible. Common sense indicates that additional practice of what is being learned in school is most often helpful for many, if not all, students. What sports coach or music teacher would say that players should not have additional practice sessions to improve the skills they will need in competitions or performances? Let's take a look at some of the arguments advanced by the critics of homework.

THE CASE AGAINST HOMEWORK

The critics of homework advance several arguments. One of the most important is that the research has not shown any significant relationship between the amount of homework students complete and their academic achievement. Alfie Kohn, in fact, says that the research has not found evidence that homework is beneficial, especially for young students. Homework is also said to penalize students who have difficulties in school. Since these students often work more slowly than other students, they end up spending more time on homework, which increases their anxiety.

The opponents of homework argue that it makes little sense to think that additional practice at home is going to help students who have difficulty understanding certain concepts or completing classroom exercises in school. Instead of helping these students catch up to their peers, the critics argue that homework actually puts them farther behind because it demoralizes the students by continually reminding them of their inability to keep up.

The critics are also quick to point out that homework takes time away from other valuable activities that students must do at home. Children need time to engage in constructive play and exercise, and they need time to be with their families. Forcing students to complete hours of homework that has no appreciable benefit would indeed be a disservice. Worse than being useless, the critics argue that homework is actually harmful because it prevents children from getting the exercise and social interaction they need to develop healthy lifestyles. And what teacher wants to be responsible for depriving children of their healthy lifestyles?

Finally, opponents point out that there are an increasing number of parents who are frustrated with the demands that homework imposes upon them. Often, these parents are frustrated because they are expected to help their children complete assignments that have not been clearly explained by the teacher. In fact, in some cases the parents are expected to teach their children things that have not been taught at school. Also, opponents note that some parents think homework intrudes on their family life, making it difficult for them to build positive relationships with their children. This growing cadre of parents is leading school boards across North America to enact regulations that seriously restrict the amount and type of homework that teachers can assign to their students.

These arguments against homework need to be responded to in a serious way. If homework does not truly benefit students, indeed, there is little reason to assign it. Teachers must be able to demonstrate that their educational practices result in high quality learning, and homework should only be assigned if it contributes to that learning.

EVALUATING THE ARGUMENTS

We acknowledge Kohn's skepticism about proving that homework is a cause of greater academic achievement. Nevertheless, some research shows that there is a positive relationship between the amount and kind of homework that students complete, within limits, and their academic achievement. Thus, we think that the homework opponents assert too strongly, and without qualification, that the research evidence contradicts the commonsense belief that homework is beneficial for students.

However, the amount of time students spend on homework is not as burdensome as some of the opponents imply. Recent research by Thomas Juster and his colleagues (2004) at the University of Michigan Institute for Social Research, for example, indicates that the average time students in elementary schools spend on homework is about twenty-two minutes per weekday, and the average time high school students spend on homework is about fifty minutes per weekday. Considering that school days are generally six hours or less, this amount of homework does not seem unreasonable for most students.

Not surprisingly, some research on homework shows a positive relationship between the amount of homework students complete, up to a limit, and their academic achievement, especially for students in middle and senior high school. We acknowledge that a positive relationship may not be evident for students in the early grades. Nevertheless, we think that the best approach is to take this evidence at face value; that is, older students receive greater benefits from doing homework than younger students. This is, in part, because older students are more capable of working independently, are better able to read and write, and are more capable of completing the work without assistance from their parents.

Even though teachers encourage young students to read at home, those who are just learning to read will probably get less benefit from completing homework assignments than Grade 12 students who have already mastered the basic skills. Moreover, older students have longer attention spans. This is why teachers assign more homework to older students than to younger students. Not surprisingly, this practice fits with the research evidence.

Common sense gives us an answer to the critics who ask why homework would ever be assigned. Simply put, spending focused time practicing a skill is the best way to improve the performance of that skill. This is why, for example, music students practice scales and rehearse music, why singers practice sight singing and rehearse vocal scores, why athletes spend hours in repetitive drills, and why student drivers spend considerable time practicing parallel parking before taking their driving test.

The most important skills people learn in life usually require practice so that they become second nature for individuals. The limited empirical evidence that we have reviewed suggests that homework is beneficial because it increases the amount of focused time that students spend on-task (see Canadian Council on Learning 2009; Cooper 2006). In other words, carefully constructed homework, at the higher grade levels, provides students with needed practice, elaboration, and expansion of the skills and understanding they have obtained from their teachers' lessons.

In addition, we challenge the idea that assigning homework to students who are having difficulty with school work is counterproductive and demoralizing. It is probably more demoralizing for students to be promoted to the next grade before they have acquired the necessary knowledge and mastered the necessary skills. The reality is that students who have more difficulty understanding certain concepts and demonstrating the required skills are more often the students who need to spend more time on assignments at both school and home. If homework assignments are properly designed, they can help students with the practice that they need to master the required concepts, knowledge, and skills.

Finally, the claim that homework takes time away from valuable recreational and family activities needs to be examined carefully. Using the same data from the study by Thomas Juster, Hiromo Ono, and Frank Stafford (2004) at the Institute for Social Research, University of Michigan, cited by some of the opponents of homework, one sees that in the United States school-aged children spend, on average, two hours watching television programs every weekday.

No doubt, many parents and teachers would agree that watching television, playing video games, and surfing the Internet are probably taking considerable time away from constructive childhood recreational and educational activities. Thus, we suggest that in most Canadian and American households, plenty of time is available for children to complete a moderate amount of homework if their parents restrict the amount of time they spend on less productive activities such as watching television or playing video games.

Given a choice between having their children work on basic math facts or writing essays and watching the latest reality television program or surfing the Internet, we think that most parents would choose the former. In general, the evidence and common sense certainly does not support authors like Alfie Kohn (2006) and Sara Bennett and Nancy Kalish (2006), who recommend that the amount of homework that students complete should be seriously reduced or banned altogether. Rather, the evidence suggests that a reasonable amount of homework is helpful for most students.

RECOMMENDATIONS

Although we are critical of the arguments advanced by some opponents of homework, we do not think that all homework is necessarily good. Most parents and teachers realize that effective homework is meaningful, even engaging, not too difficult, and not simply busywork. Moreover, they realize that practicing skills is the best way to master them, and they understand that thoughtful preparation and careful coaching by teachers makes homework more effective. Individual or group projects may be unhelpful, unfair, and may be very difficult for teachers to evaluate fairly because the students' parents may be too involved in assisting their children.

Coming home from school with a backpack full of homework does not, in itself, indicate that students are using their time wisely, learning the subject matter, or practicing the necessary skills. Also, not all parents are able or willing to help their children with homework. Therefore, we think that it makes little sense for teachers to assign homework that students are incapable of doing by themselves or that depends on group work. But just because some homework assignments are questionable does not mean that homework should be discredited altogether. Homework that reinforces and moderately extends the knowledge and skills that are being taught in school is valuable for students.

Nevertheless, we encourage parents to closely examine the homework that is being assigned to their children. Does it relate to and reinforce the knowledge and skills that they are supposed to be learning in school? Does the homework provide preparation, practice, and elaboration of the classroom work? Is the homework promptly and carefully corrected and returned or reviewed in class? If parents think that their child's homework is not consistent with the educational objectives of the school, then they should raise their concerns with the teachers and, if necessary, with the school administrators.

Clearly, working with teachers and administrators to make homework more beneficial to children is much better than, for example, lobbying the school board to enact policies that restrict the type and amount of homework teachers can assign. We think that effective teachers should not be constrained by regulations that undermine their judgment about what students need to do to learn the curriculum.

As such, parents need to support effective teachers by ensuring that their children complete their homework. The amount of time needed will depend on the age and maturity of their children and how well they are doing in their school work. Students who are not doing very well and those who work more slowly will need to spend more time doing homework. Generally, older students will have more homework to complete than younger students, but they are often more responsible for completing it without the assistance of their parents. Moreover, some parents will not be able to assist their children in completing their homework. Obviously, effective teachers keep these things in mind when they assign homework to their students.

We strongly recommend that school officials not enact policies that severely restrict the ability of teachers to assign a reasonable amount of homework. The ability of teachers to provide effective instruction requires that they must have considerable discretion in assigning homework. But obviously teachers must exercise this discretion judiciously.

Daily, weekly, weekend, and holiday restrictions on homework may be popular with some parents and school board members but, as we noted in the prologue, Tom Warner found that his board's policies prevented him from using his own good judgment to determine when homework could be assigned to his students. We think that school work that has not been completed in school, when time was given for this, must be completed at home. It should be obvious that a moderate amount of homework does not harm students, and that properly designed and marked homework assignments can be an effective part of the teaching and learning process.

BIBLIOGRAPHY

Bennett, Sara, and Nancy Kalish. 2006. *The case against homework: How homework is hurting children and what parents can do about it.* New York: Crown Publishers. Bennett and Kalish draw on their experience as parents and the research literature to argue that there is very little evidence that homework helps students become more proficient.

Canadian Council on Learning. 2009. *A systematic review of literature examining the impact of homework on academic achievement.* Ottawa, ON: Author. This report reviews eighteen empirical studies that show that a moderate amount of homework actually helps students develop the necessary skills and understanding of the subjects they are studying.

Cooper, Harris. 2006. *The battle over homework: Common ground for administrators, teachers, and parents.* Thousand Oaks, CA: Corwin Press. This book reports on the many advantages that a moderate amount of homework has for students. It also shows how administrators and teachers can establish workable policies on assigning homework to students at various grade levels.

Cooper, Harris, J. C. Robinson, and E. A. Patall. 2006. Does homework improve academic achievement? A synthesis of research, 1987–2003. *Review of Educational Research* 76 (1): 1–62. This article reviews six years of research on the relationship between the homework students complete and their academic achievement. The article illustrates that a moderate amount of homework is consistently related to improvements in students' academic achievement.

Juster, F. Thomas, Hiromo Ono, and Frank P. Stafford. 2004. *Changing times of American youth: 1981–2003.* Ann Arbor, MI: Institute for Social Research, University of Michigan. This study examines the way a large number of American youth spend their time, and shows that not much time is spent on completing homework assignments.

Kohn, Alfie. 2006. *The homework myth: Why our kids get too much of a bad thing.* New York: Da Capo Press. This book presents a strong argument in opposition to students completing homework at all grade levels.

Loveless, Tom. 2003. *How well are American students learning? With special sections on homework, charter schools, and rural school achievement.* Washington, DC: The Brookings Institution.
This report summarizes the research literature on homework and notes that American students spend relatively little time completing homework assignments. Moreover, the report indicates that a moderate amount of homework has a positive effect on students' academic achievement.

Matthews, Jay. 2006. The weak case against homework. *Washington Post.* November 21. This article effectively debunks the arguments against homework that have been made by Alfie Kohn and other romantic progressives.

Zwaagstra, Michael, and Rodney A. Clifton. 2009. *Back to the drawing board: The case for meaningful homework.* Winnipeg, MB: Frontier Centre for Public Policy. This report examines the major arguments by homework opponents and counters them with a review of the research evidence. The report concludes that a moderate amount of carefully designed homework is an important aspect of the teaching and learning process.

11

Grades Should
Reflect Achievement

PROLOGUE

Greg Taylor sighed as he looked at the small stack of papers on his desk. To-day was the deadline for a major project and less than half of his Grade 11 English students had handed in their assignments on time. He wasn't looking forward to the next few weeks because he knew that he was going to be chasing his students around and reminding them to hand in their work.

As he looked up from his desk, he saw his colleague Yolanda Walker, an-other English teacher, standing at the doorway. She indicated that she wanted to talk to him. He motioned to her to come in and have a seat.

"Are you having as much trouble as I am getting students' assignments in on time?" began Yolanda. "A bunch of my Grade 9 students are missing several assignments, and the lunch hour detentions I've been giving them haven't been working."

Greg nodded sympathetically. "You better believe I'm having difficulty. I just don't understand how the school board members think that it makes sense to prevent us from deducting marks when the students are late in handing in their assignments. The students know about this new policy, and they are taking advantage of it."

"Not only that," replied Yolanda, "but my Grade 9 students believe that grades don't matter. We already have a social promotion policy and we can't fail them. And, the K to 8 students don't receive percentage grades anymore.

I don't think those kids understand the meaning of failure. Students are spoiled, and we are spoon-feeding them because there are no consequences if they don't do the work on time."

"Well, it looks like things are going to get worse before they get better," commented Greg, as he held up the latest copy of the superintendent's quarterly newsletter, *Focus on Learning.* "According to this article, the superintendent is planning to completely overhaul high school grading practices. Beginning next year, percentage grades will be eliminated and we will only be allowed to use comments that directly relate to each of the learning outcomes."

Yolanda thought for a moment before responding. "I've heard about this change, and honestly it doesn't make much sense to me. Many of the learning outcomes the district has for English are so abstract that I don't understand how to measure them. How do we know if the students' appreciate poetry? It is much easier to give them marks or write comments about their understanding of a specific poem than it is to assess their appreciation of poetry. It is much easier to evaluate our students' grammar and punctuation than their creativity. Why are all the outcomes in English about creativity? Besides, what am I going to say to parents when they ask about their children's marks? Your daughter is very creative but she doesn't know proper grammar. Is that what I should say?

"Some of these kids want to go to college, and the better colleges want grades and standardized achievement test scores. The only categories we're going to be allowed to use on report cards are: Not yet meeting performance standards, Meeting performance standards with assistance, Meeting performance standards, and Exceeding performance standards. I don't know what that range indicates, so how are the kids and their parents to know? How is this scheme of representing achievement any better than percentages or letter grades anyway?"

"Don't worry," replied Greg, sarcasm dripping from his voice, "according to the newsletter, we have another assessment guru coming to speak at our in-service next month. Apparently he will tell us how this new system for evaluating students will solve our problem."

"This is ridiculous," stated Yolanda. "It's already hard enough for me to explain to parents why I'm not enforcing deadlines and why I am not docking marks when the students plagiarize. I don't need to know more about idealistic assessment practices that don't really work. Why does the superintendent keep pushing this stuff on us? Doesn't she realize that we're losing credibility among the kids and their parents? Doesn't she realize that the college admission officers roll their eyes when they receive our students' transcripts? I wish the school board members would tell us why they think these new policies are such good ideas."

Greg nodded his head in agreement, "Maybe it's time that we start saying something to the superintendent. Our administrators need to know that we've had enough of these crazy ideas. They are making it impossible for us to evaluate our students' academic work properly."

INTRODUCTION

Greg and Yolanda, two committed teachers with many years of experience, have a right to be frustrated with the new policies being implemented in their school district. Their professional responsibility and discretion as teachers are being eroded by a grading scheme that is being forced on them. For the parents they are trying to communicate with, the policy seems to defy common sense. Nevertheless, many school districts in North America are adopting policies that replace traditional grading practices based on percentages and letter grades with new practices generally based on anecdotal comments and performance scales.

In our view, these policies are questionable because they weaken the connection between what the students actually do and the grades they receive. Psychologists call this relationship between performances and grades "contingency." The new grading policies advocated by some districts suggest that contingency is not important, though in most aspects of life it makes sense to have rewards that are related to the performances of individuals. While assessment gurus such as Ken O'Connor (2007), in *A Repair Kit for Grading*, and Richard Stiggins (1997), in *Student-Centered Classroom Assessment*, claim that they want to help teachers make their assessments of students better, the reality is that some of their suggestions are unreasonable and impractical.

PROBLEMS WITH SOME MODERN ASSESSMENT PRACTICES

The new grading policies that some school boards have implemented, based on the ideas of O'Connor (2007) and Stiggins (1997), often restrict the ways that teachers can evaluate their students' achievement. That is, the policies often say that teachers ought not deduct marks when students submit assignments late or assign zeros when students fail to hand in their work, they ought not penalize students for academic dishonesty, and they ought not use percentage or letter grades. Our review of these recommended practices suggests that they may not be that helpful to teachers, students, or parents.

1. Having No Penalties for Late or Missed Assignments

O'Connor (2007), for example, claims that teachers should deduct as few marks as possible—preferably none—for late assignments. In O'Connor's mind, teachers should only evaluate assignments on whether or not the students have met the specified outcomes, not the time it takes them to complete the assignments because the time to complete assignments is not generally identified as a specified learning outcome. Consequently, he says that the assessment of assignments should focus on the students' academic work and not on their adherence to artificially created deadlines.

A related but distinctive feature of assessment policies being adopted by some school districts is that zeros (or "zap") aren't permitted in evaluating students' work. If students have not completed some assignments, their teachers are not allowed to award them zeros, nor are they allowed to include these missing assignments in calculating the students' grades. Instead, if students have incomplete assignments, teachers are required to use a temporary grade of I (Incomplete) or H (Held), indicating that they will have additional time to submit the assignments. The key point of this policy is not to punish students but to inform them and their parents that some assignments are still incomplete.

School boards and senior administrators go too far when they forbid teachers from deducting marks from students who hand their assignments in late or who do not hand them in at all. Where such policies are used, teachers are finding that an increasing number of students disregard the deadlines, treating them as artificial. Without enforceable deadlines, or with weak penalties for missing deadlines, a few students submit a large number of assignments as late as the end of the school year, and expect their teachers to mark them before completing their year-end report cards. Surely such practices are unreasonable, given all the responsibilities of teachers.

If O'Connor (2007) means to suggest that teachers should focus their assessment primarily on the work that students complete and not the time it takes them to finish and submit their work, we agree. Moreover, teachers should recognize that there are times when students are unable to complete assignments by the deadline, and it may be unfair to arbitrarily deduct marks from them. But it is also sensible for teachers to examine the consequences of having no penalties for late or missed assignments. We think it is reasonable to assume that effective teachers will, in fact, use their discretion to take account of the genuine reasons students have for tardiness, given their age, maturity, and other specific circumstances.

Common sense suggests that a policy of no penalties for late or missed assignments should only apply for a reasonable length of time and should not be used to permit students to hand in assignments at any time they please. This is unfair to both teachers and students. The timeliness of assignments and the impact of missed assignments on grades must clearly be in the teachers' hands because the pace of instruction, including assignments and their correction, and any remedial lessons that teachers judge necessary, must be timely, along with the students' knowledge of how well they are doing throughout the course. Also, having assignments completed on time will help students keep up to date with their school work, which is a distinct advantage to them.

2. Penalizing Dishonest Students

One of the strangest suggestions to become policy concerns academic dishonesty. O'Connor (2007) actually says that students who are caught copying the work of others should not be punished by having their grades reduced. Moreover, he recommends that teachers should prevent cheating by making their assignments more interesting and ensuring that students are properly taught about plagiarism.

We think that reasonable people would agree with the emphasis on prevention; certainly we do—teachers have a responsibility to teach students what they need to know and they need to do this in interesting ways, as we pointed out elsewhere. Academic honesty is a value worthy of teachers' direct attention; knowing how to cite the work of others properly is a skill that should be an explicit part of the instruction in writing essays and reports.

But, O'Connor (2007) goes on to say that, even after proper instruction, if teachers discover students have cheated, they should interview the students privately and require that they redo the assignments. Reasonable people might well disagree with this suggestion because they see it as an unreasonable indulgence. Teachers do not have unlimited time to review and correct assignments that students have plagiarized.

While teachers need to be able to use their professional discretion in grading assignments that have been plagiarized, it is equally obvious that teachers need to warn students that colleges and universities are not likely to be lenient with those who plagiarize. As such, teachers must convey the view that academic dishonesty is a serious offense and is usually met with serious academic penalties.

3. Replacing Percentages and Letter Grades with Performance Scales

In some school jurisdictions, teachers are not permitted to use letter grades or percentages; instead, they are required to use other schemes such as the four-point categorical scale recommended by O'Connor (2007), with the following descriptors: (1) not yet meeting performance standards, (2) meeting performance standards with assistance, (3) meeting performance standards, and (4) exceeding performance standards.

More significantly, O'Connor (2007) recommends that teachers should assess many objectives for every assignment in every subject. Thus, for example, instead of assigning a percentage or letter grade for an essay, teachers would identify a large number of specific objectives and evaluate essays on each of them. For teachers, this would often prove to be overwhelming in complexity, details, and the time required.

In addition, this complexity is not likely to make reporting achievement easier or more accurate for students or their parents because they will need to know the answer to a number of important questions. What knowledge and skills need to be shown by students to improve from one category to the next? How much assistance is being provided? Will sufficient independence be developed by the student to warrant promotion to the next grade? Is the performance minimal or beyond it? How do students and parents know? Obviously, an evaluation system based on standards requires that they be explicit for every subject at every grade level—can these be communicated effectively to students and parents?

Teachers and parents will recognize that any scheme for evaluating and reporting achievement raises important questions; indeed, it is supposed to do that. But it is not obvious that novelty in evaluation and reporting schemes is an advantage, or that complexity and detail make them necessarily superior to more conventional ones. In many situations, percentages and letter grades have the advantage of being familiar and well understood, and can convey students' achievement with considerable precision. For example, students and parents easily understand that a grade of 50 percent is usually a pass, and that 95 percent is outstanding. Fundamentally, percentages and letter grades should not be hastily discarded.

RECOMMENDATIONS

To have a better understanding of our concerns, we need to return to the fundamental reasons for assessing students. To be effective, teachers must know how to focus their instruction to meet the diversity of their students' knowledge and skills. Also, teachers have to evaluate their students' learning against mandated standards of achievement. Furthermore, they need to communicate the results of their evaluations to the students themselves, to their parents, and to other teachers and administrators, as necessary.

We urge classroom teachers to make sure their grading practices are relatively simple, appropriate to the subject and grade, and understandable by the students and their parents. Teachers should use a variety of assignments and tests in evaluating their students so they have greater confidence in the final grades that students receive. The weightings of the various assignments should be clearly explained to students and parents. We do not think that these requirements are too burdensome for teachers. Teachers should not be overly rigid or, indeed, too flexible in grading their students, and should be cautious in assigning zeros or docking marks for late assignments unless there are good reasons for doing so. Clearly, incomplete work cannot be tolerated indefinitely. But these decisions are fundamentally instructional ones and are best left to teachers, within the framework of a school policy.

Parents, specifically, deserve to receive accurate and readily understandable information on the achievement and progress of their children. They should not receive report cards with information that is difficult for them to interpret. Of course, we are not opposed to teachers providing additional information that places the students' performances in a broader context. The range of scores and the average achievement of students writing examinations, for example, would be helpful.

Generally, we encourage parents to examine carefully the report cards their children bring home, and if they cannot understand how their children are being graded, they should ask their teachers to explain their grading scheme and justify the marks that their children received. If they remain unsatisfied, then they should take their concerns to the principal, parental advisory committee, and the school board, as necessary. Finally, we urge senior educational administrators to consider the merits of a common and largely conventional grading scheme for use throughout the school district.

BIBLIOGRAPHY

Airasian, Peter W., Joseph F. Engemann, and Tiffany L. Gallagher. 2007. *Classroom assessment: Concepts and applications.* Toronto: McGraw-Hill Ryerson.
This is an excellent textbook on constructing assessment instruments and the ways teachers can make sure that their grades reflect their students' achievement.

American Psychological Association. 1995. *Standards for educational and psychological testing.* Washington, DC: Author.
These standards have been prepared by a joint committee of the American Educational Research Association, the American Psychological Association, and the National Council on Measurement in Education, and they cover the construction of tests, reliability, validity, and fairness in the interpretation of tests. Teachers and administrators, in both Canada and the United States, should be familiar with these standards.

Holmes, Mark. 1993. *The educator's guide to student evaluation.* Toronto: OISE Press.
This book was written for teachers, but it is a useful guide for parents who want to understand the principles underlying the assessment of their children's achievement.

Koretz, Daniel. 2009. *Measuring up: What educational testing really tells us.* Cambridge, MA: Harvard University Press.
This book was awarded The American Association of Colleges for Teacher Education Outstanding Book Award in 2009. Koretz examines problems with educational testing. He pays particular attention to how test scores can be misinterpreted.

McMillan, James H. 2007. *Classroom assessment: Principles and practice for effective standards-based instruction.* 4th ed. Boston, MA: Allyn and Bacon.
This is an excellent book for teachers on the importance of assessment in teaching and learning, creating high-quality classroom assessment instruments, and interpreting the results properly.

Nitko, Anthony J. 2004. *Educational assessment of students.* 4th ed. Upper Saddle River, NJ: Pearson Prentice Hall.
This book provides a balanced review of virtually all the important issues for teachers to understand when they assess their students.

O'Connor, Ken. 2007. *A repair kit for grading: Fifteen fixes for broken grades.*
Portland, OR: Assessment Testing Institute.
This book offers a number of suggestions for reforming traditional grading
practices. Although some of the prescriptions are useful, many are impractical.

Stiggins, Richard J. 1997. *Student-centered classroom assessment.* 2nd ed. Upper
Saddle River, NJ: Prentice Hall.
This book encourages teachers to be much more student-centered in their
assessment practices.

A Pass Should Be Earned

"Okay class, open your math books and turn to page fifty-three. We're going to correct the twenty algebra questions that were due for today. Get out a red pen and pass your assignment to the student behind you," directed Edward Sinclair, a Grade 8 mathematics and science teacher at Alfred Street Middle School.

As students began passing back their papers, Mr. Sinclair noticed that one student, Tyler Reimer, had nothing on his desk. Mr. Sinclair walked over to his desk and leaned over to speak to him. "Where are your assignment notebook and your textbook, Tyler?" he asked.

"I dunno," mumbled Tyler in response. "I guess I forgot everything at home."

Mr. Sinclair sighed in exasperation. This was not the first time he had heard this response from Tyler. "Tyler, at least half of your assignments are still incomplete and your last test mark was not promising. If you don't start completing your homework, you're not going to pass this course," he warned.

Tyler shrugged his shoulders. He had heard it all before. "Look Mr. Sinclair, I don't like math, and besides, I know you have to pass me anyway. That's what happens in this school."

Hearing this Mr. Sinclair was somewhat irritated but tried not to show it. "Tyler, your attitude is not helpful. Math is important and you need to finish your assignments. You can't expect to succeed in Grade 9 if you don't do the work in Grade 8. Please see me at the end of the period." Before allowing himself to become even more frustrated, Edward Sinclair turned and walked to the front of the room to resume reviewing the assigned work with the students who had completed it.

When the school day ended, Edward Sinclair headed to the office to speak with the vice-principal, Maria Jacobs. There was no one else in her office, and Maria invited Edward to have a seat and asked him what was on his mind.

"I'm concerned about Tyler Reimer," he began. "He's not putting much effort into completing his assignments, and he has absolutely no chance of passing math. But, it is his attitude that is disturbing because when I warned him that he is in danger of failing Grade 8, he shrugged and said he will pass no matter how much work he does."

Maria paused briefly before responding. "Well, I agree that his attitude needs to improve. But he's right about not failing Grade 8. The school board recently implemented a no-fail policy that prevents students from being held back. Don't you know that research proves that grade retention is more harmful than helpful to students?" concluded Maria.

"That's ridiculous!" exploded Edward. "How can the research show that it is helpful to promote students in subjects like math when they cannot understand the work? How can we keep passing kids like Tyler who don't meet the grade-level standards? If they know that they will be passed automatically, isn't our policy encouraging them to take advantage of the system? Is this what we favor? And why would parents think this is a good idea?"

At this point, Maria stood up to indicate that the discussion was over. "I know that you disagree with this policy. But at the end of the day, Tyler Reimer is not going to be retained in Grade 8. It's our professional responsibility to make our courses engaging enough so that all the students, including Tyler, want to learn. Make whatever adaptations are necessary to ensure that Tyler succeeds," ended Maria.

Edward left Maria's office in frustration, thinking to himself: "I can't believe how low our standards have become! How does passing kids who don't know the material help them in the next grade? How does this prepare our students for college and life in the real world? Employers certainly don't have to make work interesting; it just needs to get done."

INTRODUCTION

Edward Sinclair has good reason to be frustrated. In Alfred Street Middle School, students no longer need to meet specific academic standards to pass to the next grade; all students are promoted from grade to grade regardless of their effort or their achievement. To cope with the challenges this policy creates, the teachers are expected to adapt their teaching and assessment methods to accommodate a wide range of abilities, levels of achievement, and interests.

While it is legitimate to ask teachers to be adaptive, there is a limit to what they can reasonably be expected to do. Where the actual achievement of the students does not matter much, the educational system lacks credibility. Where the final achievement of a reasonable standard is not required of virtually all students, it is not surprising that a number of conscientious teachers, like Edward Sinclair, will become frustrated and disillusioned.

We wish we could say that Alfred Street Middle School is a fictitious school that bears little resemblance to most public schools in North America. In fact, social promotion has become a common practice, whether explicitly as policy or subtly as pressure on teachers to make sure that all students pass. We need to take a closer look at it.

THE CASE FOR SOCIAL PROMOTION

Advocates who support social promotion tend to focus on the problems they think are associated with the failing of students. For example, they often claim that forcing children to repeat a grade while their friends and classmates progress to the next grade is socially and emotionally devastating and leads to increased personal, behavioral, and academic problems. They believe promoting failing students so they remain with their classmates avoids these problems. In other words, it is more important for children to stay with their peers than to meet specified performance standards in particular grades.

These advocates claim that the research shows that students who are retained frequently experience short-term academic gains, but the improvements tend to fade after three or four years. The initial benefits of retention are temporary; consequently, advocates of social promotion contend that, in the long run, students are better off if they are promoted along with their classmates.

In addition, advocates of social promotion argue that retaining students increases the cost of their education. Promoting weak students and providing academic support to them is said to be more cost-effective than retention. Thus, the need to protect the self-esteem of weak students, the claim that long-term gains in academic performance rarely result from grade retention, and the financial cost of retaining students in a grade for a second year are the main reasons why many educators and school boards appear to favor social promotion. Are these reasons valid?

THE CASE AGAINST SOCIAL PROMOTION

The reasons for social promotion appear persuasive, but an examination of the research literature leads us to question the basic claims. The claim that research has proven that social promotion is better than retention is, at best, ambiguous. The Beginning School Study, a long-term research project conducted in Baltimore, examined the academic and emotional effects of retention on a large number of students during their first eight years in school. The results of this study were published in *On the Success of Failure* by Karl Alexander, Doris Entwisle, and Susan Dauber (2003). They report that the negative emotional effects of grade retention on students were substantially less than expected, and that the children who were retained normally experienced long-term, rather than short-term, increases in academic achievement.

In a recent rigorous analysis of the grade retention and promotion research, Jon Lorence (2009) says: "Contrary to the prevailing wisdom among educational researchers, there is no overwhelming body of evidence which conclusively demonstrates that making low performing students repeat a grade harms their later academic achievement. Although opponents of retention will strongly disagree with this assessment . . . an examination of more recent research does not appear to resolve the issue" (1166).

As a careful researcher, Lorence (2009) is, of course, concerned with whether or not these results are trustworthy. In this respect he registers an important specific concern: "A comprehensive examination of the grade retention literature reveals a far more exacting standard of what constitutes 'acceptable research' is applied to studies which support the practice of grade retention" (1167). However, research "concluding that grade retention is an ineffective remediation practice is not subjected to the higher standards of methodological rigor required" (1167).

What might explain this difference? Lorence (2009) cites the same explanation as Alexander, Entwisle, and Dauber (2003, 16–20), namely that "educational researchers have such strong opinions on the subject of grade retention that they are biased against any evidence which contradicts the view that holding students back a year in grade is bad educational practice" (1167). The results of this review of the research literature suggest that many educators have been too quick to dismiss the merits of keeping weak or struggling students in a grade for an additional year.

Perhaps this is a good time to set aside claims that "my research is better than your research" and use some common sense. In the prologue, Tyler has figured out that no matter what he does, he will be promoted. He knows that he does not need to pass mathematics, or any other course, to be promoted to Grade 9. Tyler is not thinking about the difficulty he may have in Grade 9 because he is only thinking about staying with his friends. Since he dislikes mathematics, why should he work hard when he is guaranteed to pass?

Consequently, the classroom teacher, Edward Sinclair, has to cajole and coerce Tyler to do his work. We ask the advocates of social promotion these questions: what is more important—Tyler's self-esteem or his academic achievement? Even if both are considered important, should we ignore Tyler's conclusions about the value of his efforts and his academic performance? Perhaps social promotion encourages students to devalue effort and achievement, an outcome we surely do not want.

Or just imagine what would happen if driver education instructors adopted social promotion policies. Suppose all student drivers received their licenses regardless of whether or not they knew how to drive a car or knew the rules of the road. Think of the harm done to the self-esteem of young drivers who failed to pass their driver's exam and were unable to drive at the same time as their peers. Yes, indeed, it would be embarrassing for some adolescents to fail their tests. But any loss of self-esteem or embarrassment that these adolescents may feel is better than the alternative of having incompetent drivers.

Given the arguments that have been made about social promotion, we suspect that research studies, if there were any, would show that drivers who had to repeat their driving exams would be more likely to have problems in driving than those who passed them on the first attempt. The studies might even show that the failures of some students gave rise to considerable emotional disturbance and frustration. These student drivers may well have been embarrassed and frustrated, and they may even have lower self-esteem.

Would people be prepared to accept social promotion in driver education programs simply to preserve the self-esteem of adolescents? We think not. Being certain that people learn how to drive safely is more important than their embarrassment, frustration, or self-esteem. Ensuring that they receive a driver's license, regardless of their knowledge or driving ability, would severely undermine the credibility of the license.

Why do we expect less from public schools than from driving schools? Don't all schools exist to ensure that students have the knowledge and skills they are supposed to possess and are certified as possessing? Surely, there must be specific ways of knowing that students actually possess the required knowledge and skills at certain levels of proficiency.

Allowing students to enter the next grade in school, regardless of their performance, undermines the credibility of the public education system, something that is not allowed to happen in driving schools. What value would there be to a high school diploma when it no longer meant that certain standards had been attained? Obviously, public education is at least as important as driver education, and consequently high school diplomas must have at least the same value and credibility.

Another argument supporting social promotion is that it is less costly than grade retention because of the added expense of providing additional education for students who fail a grade. We agree that it costs thousands of dollars to educate a single student for a year, and estimates suggest that retaining one student for one year increases the total cost of educating that student by about 10 percent. However, the main purpose of schooling is to educate students, not to save money. Perhaps the long-term cost to society of graduates who fail to meet basic academic standards may be greater than the short-term cost of providing additional years of education for them. But this really is a research question about which we have very little evidence, and we need much more (Lorence 2009).

Recall in the prologue that Mr. Sinclair was rightly disappointed and frustrated with Tyler's effort and achievement in mathematics. Also, remember that he did not receive assistance from the vice principal, Maria Jacobs, and that the district policy was equally unhelpful. Here, we ask: should we count as trivial Edward Sinclair's frustration with a policy of social promotion that undermines his instructional decisions and professional judgment?

In fact, we think that social promotion often places unrealistic demands on teachers. When students are promoted from grade to grade without first mastering the requisite skills and knowledge in the previous grade, teachers are expected to adapt to this fact in their instruction and evaluation. As these students continue from grade to grade, the diversity in the classroom is likely to increase, and this means that teachers are likely to have increasing difficulty in providing suitable instruction for all the students. This greater classroom diversity can be attributed to social promotion, and we think it is an unfair burden on teachers.

Finally, we ask if social promotion prepares students for life. In what postsecondary institution, workplace, or profession do all people get regular promotions regardless of their motivation, effort, or achievement? Obviously, when students know that they will be passed from grade to grade even when they have failed to meet the required standards, they receive very poor preparation for life as a citizen.

Simply, social promotion sends the wrong message because it tells students that their effort and achievement matter less than remaining with their peers. We think that Grade 8 is not too early for Tyler Reimer and most other students to begin learning some real-world lessons. Our position is not that grade retention is a perfect solution, but we think it is preferable for the reasons and arguments we have presented. Essentially, we think that standards of achievement matter, and when schools certify that students are academically proficient, they should do so responsibly.

RECOMMENDATIONS

Social promotion is a misguided policy that undermines the effort that many teachers rightly make to sustain academic standards. As a result, we strongly urge school boards, superintendents, and school administrators not to embrace strict no-fail policies. While it is appropriate for teachers to, within reason, help their students acquire the knowledge and skills that are necessary for them to pass onto the next grade, students need to make a reasonable effort to learn.

Education is, in fact, a cooperative endeavor in which teachers and students must work together. Sometimes teachers work diligently to help students, but the students may not do much to help themselves. In such situations, students must be held accountable for their lack of effort. We recognize, of course, that the lack of ability is a different matter.

Instead, educational authorities should enact policies that help teachers do what is best for their students. There are times where retaining students in their current grade would be appropriate because of serious academic deficiencies or because they have not put in the required effort. Similarly, there are times when students have fallen slightly short of the standards for being promoted to the next grade, but they have worked hard throughout the year and have shown promising improvements. If the teachers are confident that the deficiencies can be remediated, perhaps by tutorial study or summer school, there may be good reason for promoting these students.

But this decision should be made in light of a realistic prognosis of the child's probable success, and it should be made by the teachers and the principal in consultation with the students' parents, so that the advantages, disadvantages, and rationale of particular decisions can be understood and appreciated by everyone concerned. The key is that teachers and principals, and indeed parents, should not be tied to rigid policies that foreclose options and flexibility. Rather, in circumstances where retention is being considered, the guiding principle should be the honest, realistic, and timely communication of assessments from the school to the parents. The avoidance of rigid policies, substantial deference to professional judgment, and candid communication and consultation with parents should be seen as requirements that are justified by common sense.

But parents have specific responsibilities, too. In schools with no-fail policies or conventions, parents must realize that it is best if their children meet grade-level standards before they are promoted. This means that parents may need to tell the educational officials that they do not favor social promotion or no-fail policies.

In schools where retention is possible, and except for those cases where a modification of curricular standards is justified by the need to accommodate certain limitations in the child's capacities, parents should not expect teachers to promote their children if they have not reached a reasonable standard of proficiency. Obviously, we believe that a pass should be earned by virtually all students, and promotion should certify the student's considerable success, and it should be an occasion for the celebration of accomplishment as much by the teachers and school administrators as by the student and the parent.

BIBLIOGRAPHY

Alexander, Karl L., Doris R. Entwisle, and Susan L. Dauber. 2003. *On the success of failure: A reassessment of the effects of retention in the primary grades.* New York: Cambridge University Press.
This book reports a careful study of the emotional and academic effects of grade retention on students and shows that retention is often beneficial.

Clifton, Rodney A. 2002. A modified voucher system and public school accountability. *Journal of Thought* 37 (Fall): 25–32.
This article proposes that if students fall two grades below grade level, school boards should provide a voucher to parents so they can obtain remedial education from private tutors. This policy would encourage teachers and principals to keep students from falling below grade level.

Lorence, Jon. 2009. Grade retention redux: A dissenting perspective. In *International handbook of research on teachers and teaching,* ed. Lawerence J. Saha and A. Gary Dworkin, 1153–75. New York: Springer.
This chapter reviews the research literature on retaining and promoting students from grade to grade. The author notes that retaining students for a second year is not as harmful as many educators and administrators seem to believe.

Mandzuk, David. 1995. Does research tell the whole story? Taking another look at social promotion. In *Crosscurrents: Contemporary Canadian educational issues,* ed. Lance W. Roberts and Rodney A. Clifton, 181–87. Scarborough, ON: Nelson Canada.
This chapter, written by a practicing teacher, examines the research evidence for social promotion and notes that there are substantial difficulties in fairly implementing no-fail policies in schools.

Smith, Mary L., and Lorrie A. Shepard. 1987. What doesn't work: Explaining policies of retention in the early grades. *Phi Delta Kappan* (October): 129–34.
This article contains many arguments against grade retention and in favor of social promotion.

III

SOME THINGS
ARE DISTRACTING

Teachers' Unions Don't Always Put Students First

PROLOGUE

"Welcome to our school, Mr. Patterson," began Jerome King, a Grade 6 teacher at Redwood Elementary School. "I'm glad that you were able to stop by on your way home from work."

"No problem, I was going to pick Natasha up from school anyway," replied Alberto Patterson. "The note that Natasha brought home said you wanted to speak to me about a very important matter. My wife and I take a very active role in our daughter's education and we always meet with her teachers. I certainly want to hear what your concerns are."

Jerome motioned to Alberto to have a seat. "You have probably heard about some of the so-called reforms that the Department of Education is planning to implement."

Alberto replied that he was somewhat familiar with the proposed changes, but hadn't been reading the newspaper articles that closely. Nevertheless, he was wondering what this had to do with his daughter.

"Our professional association is very concerned with these changes," continued Jerome. "One of our biggest concerns is with the plan to implement standardized testing at the end of Grades 3, 6, 9, and 12 in the core subjects. As professionals, our association believes that standardized testing will be harmful to Natasha's education."

Alberto was a little confused by what he was hearing. "Actually, it seems to me that this kind of testing is probably a good idea. It's just a normal part of education, isn't it? Wouldn't these tests help give us a better idea of how our kids are doing in the core subjects? What could be wrong with getting more information about the academic progress of our kids?

Jerome seemed irritated by Alberto's comment, but he caught himself quickly. "Some parents have misconceptions about standardized tests. Many educational experts have shown that authentic assessment is a much better way to find out how well the students are doing. Standardized tests measure one thing and only one thing, how well kids can take tests."

Jerome paused as if expecting Alberto to interject a comment. When he didn't, Jerome continued. "Our professional association is gathering signatures from teachers and parents on a petition, and we are planning to send it to the government. Many parents are supporting the teachers, and I was hoping that you would sign the petition, too," concluded Jerome.

"So that was why you asked me to come and see you?" asked Alberto incredulously. "Were we going to talk about my daughter at all?"

"Natasha is doing very well, and I don't have any concerns about her work," responded Jerome. "However, the government is planning a number of changes that will seriously undermine the professional autonomy of Natasha's teachers. Our petition will help make sure that she continues to receive the excellent education that she is receiving now."

Alberto had heard enough. "I'm sorry Mr. King. I came to meet with you to talk about how my daughter is doing in school. I'm not prepared to sign any petition until I have given it some thought. I want to talk with other parents first."

"If you decide to sign the petition," said Jerome, "please let me know by the end of the week when the petition will be sent to the government. I really think it is important for parents and teachers to work together on these common issues. And, the education of your daughter is very important to both of us."

Alberto quickly thanked Jerome for being concerned about his daughter's education, met Natasha in the hall, gave her a big hug, and went out the door to the parking lot. On the drive home, Alberto thought about the meeting and wondered whether he should sign the petition. "I'm going to look into this matter more closely," he thought. "Something doesn't seem right. I don't think that Jerome's union should be asking me to sign petitions."

INTRODUCTION

Does Alberto have a good reason to be concerned about the petition from the teachers' union opposing standardized testing? After all, Jerome is an excellent teacher who says that the only thing teachers want is the best education for their students. The teachers' union, which is made up of teachers like Jerome, has taken a strong stand against the testing proposed by the government. If the teachers actually have the best interests of their students in mind, isn't the union's opposition to standardized tests the right decision? If so, shouldn't parents support the union and oppose the testing proposal?

Not necessarily, is the answer to both these questions; the union's opposition to the tests is not necessarily in the interests of students or parents, and the union's expectation of parental support is not necessarily reasonable. It is important to realize that teachers' unions, like all unions, exist primarily to promote the welfare of their members, and they receive all of their money from their members' dues. Therefore, it is logical that the interests of teachers' unions can differ from those of students and parents, and it is misleading for teachers' unions to claim, as some do, that they put students' interests first. A brief examination of the typical stance of teachers' unions on some key issues of educational reform will demonstrate this point.

TEACHERS' UNIONS AND EDUCATIONAL REFORM

In the prologue, Jerome King's union opposes the government's plan to have students write standardized tests and it is asking parents to support this position. Such tests would require teachers, like Jerome, to stick more closely to the prescribed curriculum because the test would assess their students' understanding of it. Jerome's union argues that these tests undermine the autonomy of teachers perhaps because they would have less control over the curriculum and the evaluation of their students.

Are standardized tests good for students? As we explained in chapter 2, standardized tests represent an important way of ensuring that all students in similar circumstances study the same curriculum, have a comparable opportunity to learn it, and are evaluated on the same basis. As a form of assessment, they allow students' achievement to be compared fairly with students in other schools across the province, state, country, or internationally.

Standardized tests also help counter the inequity for students of different teachers having different standards of evaluation. In other words, standardized tests based on a mandated curriculum present a valid and reliable measurement of the students' academic achievement. When the results of standardized tests are available, students and parents receive valuable information about the students' academic performance in comparison with other students in the same subject and grade.

Unfortunately, teachers' unions have often been hostile to standardized testing, and their arguments are typically couched in language that suggests that they speak for the best interests of students. Opinion surveys—the one conducted by Neil Guppy and his associates (2005), for example—indicate that most parents and many teachers support the use of standardized exams, showing that many teachers disagree with their unions. Therefore, parents and teachers need to think for themselves when the unions claim that using standardized exams are not in the best interests of students' education.

An actual case illustrates our words of caution. The British Columbia Teachers' Federation (BCTF) represents forty-three thousand public school teachers in the province. Since 2000, the provincial government has required all Grade 4 and Grade 7 students to participate in the Foundation Skills Assessment (FSA), a program of standardized tests of the basic academic skills in reading, writing, and mathematics.

Even though these tests provide valuable information about the students' academic achievement, the BCTF stridently urges its members to refuse to administer the tests to their students. Also, the BCTF has sent letters and brochures to parents urging them to request that their children be exempted from the FSA. One brochure contains a prepared letter opposing the FSA and asks parents to sign their names and send the letter to the provincial government. These tactics show how some teachers' unions try to persuade both teachers and parents to support causes that the union leadership favors.

Similarly, teachers' unions have objected to policies that would allow parents to have greater choice in selecting the schools their children attend. In jurisdictions where parents have a greater choice of schools, such as where vouchers are used and charter schools are available, the performance of many students has improved, partly because parents were not forced to send their children to underperforming schools, as Jay Greene (2005) demonstrates in *Education Myths: What Special Interest Groups Want You to Believe about Our Schools—and Why It Isn't So.*

When coupled with publicly available test scores, vouchers have given many parents the information and resources they need in deciding whether to enroll their children in other schools. Obviously, vouchers enable low-income parents to have the very choices that already exist for wealthy parents who can afford to live in neighborhoods with good schools or to send their children to private schools.

Nevertheless, the National Education Association (NEA), the largest teachers' union in the United States, officially opposes the use of vouchers. On its website, the NEA lays out a number of reasons why it believes teachers, parents, and other concerned citizens should not support the use of vouchers. Specifically, the NEA argues that vouchers harm the public school system by encouraging students to enroll in private schools, and they provide little benefit to disadvantaged students. But Greene (2005, 178) exhaustively reviews the evidence and concludes: "The evidence from existing voucher programs consistently shows public schools improving in response to the challenge of vouchers. [We] are not aware of any study that shows U.S. public school test scores declining in response to vouchers."

Why do teachers' unions often oppose school choice and vouchers? Very likely it is because allowing parental choice reduces the number of students attending public schools, decreasing the jobs available for union members. The unions generally ignore the findings of Greene (2005), which could reasonably be understood as beneficial to students and parents.

In fact, teachers' unions have a monopoly in the Canadian provinces and virtually a monopoly in most U.S. states. They benefit enormously from education systems that make it difficult for parents to remove their children from poor schools and send them to better schools. Requiring all students to attend designated public schools ensures that funding remains relatively stable and consequently the jobs of teachers remain secure. Furthermore, any demand for achievement data that allows the comparison of schools can be opposed by teachers' unions as being simply unnecessary. In their view, all schools are good schools; none are better than any other.

Probably the most serious conflict between the interests of teachers' unions and the interests of students and parents concerns performance-based pay for teachers. Teachers' unions, with a few notable exceptions, are strongly opposed to paying teachers on the basis of their performance, the measurement of which would obviously include the achievement of their students. Even though virtually every other profession has some form of performance-based pay, teachers' unions stubbornly cling to a salary scale based on the teachers' years of teaching experience and their years of postsecondary education.

Over the past decade, however, considerable evidence has shown that there is little, if any, relationship between these two factors and the actual achievement of the teachers' students. Yet teachers' unions have been very successful in protecting their members from any changes to the structure of compensation. No one begrudges teachers' unions trying to get higher salaries for their members, but not at any price. If some teachers are better at instructing students than others, it makes sense that they should be paid more, but the structure of compensation that is embedded in virtually all collective agreements prevents this. However, if the more effective teachers stay in teaching while the less effective leave, the achievement of students would improve and parents would likely be more satisfied.

Many people may be inclined to believe teachers' unions when they claim that increasing spending on public education obviously benefits students. However, per-pupil funding levels vary quite substantially across the Canadian provinces and the U.S. states, and there is little, if any, evidence that increasing per-pupil funding, of itself, increases the academic achievement of students. In some jurisdictions, increasing funding merely increases the size and complexity of the school district bureaucracy; in other jurisdictions, increasing the funding simply increases the salaries of the teachers already employed; and in other jurisdictions, increasing funding may lead to new teachers being hired.

The hiring of new teachers may be related to the campaign of teacher unions for limits on the number of students in a classroom. Indeed, some collective agreements stipulate maximum class sizes. Teachers' unions contend that smaller classes lead to higher academic achievement by students, fewer behavioral problems, and more manageable workloads for teachers.

Undoubtedly, these policies make teachers' lives easier. While this may be an important goal, the evidence that reducing class size always improves academic achievement of students is weak, unless the reduction is to fifteen or fewer students (Greene 2005). In fact, in jurisdictions where class size has been reduced modestly, most notably in Tennessee and California, the effect on the academic achievement of students has been minimal, in part because the policy limiting class size required the district to build new classrooms and to hire more teachers, some of whom were less qualified (Greene 2005, 49–57).

Additionally, Peter Brimelow (2003) notes that in the first two years of California's class-size-reduction initiative, the California Teachers' Association saw its dues-paying membership increase by 12 percent because an additional thirty-seven thousand new teachers were hired. Thus, it isn't surprising that teachers' unions support legislating smaller class sizes when more teachers become union members and substantial benefits are realized by the union. There is nothing wrong with teachers' unions looking after their members' interests, but there is something wrong in the union's claiming that improving the education of students is their primary concern. As such, citizens, including individual teachers, must recognize the specific interests that are being served when teachers' unions advance or resist certain educational reforms.

Nevertheless, some teachers' unions in the United States have been willing to embrace reforms that, in fact, improve the education of students as described in Karen Litzcke's (2001) *Teachers Unions as Players in Education Reform*. For example, the American Federation of Teachers (AFT), which is the country's second largest teachers' union, supports rigorous national curriculum standards. In a *Washington Post* editorial, AFT president Randi Weingarten (2009) sounded a lot like E. D. Hirsch Jr. when she explained the importance of ensuring that all students learn a common core of knowledge and skills: "Education is a local issue, but there is a body of knowledge about what children should know and be able to do that should guide decisions about curriculum and testing."

Previous AFT presidents, most notably the late Albert Shanker, have also acknowledged that teachers' unions need to support ideas that they once opposed if they wish to remain relevant to parents and students. The willingness of the AFT to embrace core knowledge principles and policies that promote educational excellence should be recognized and encouraged by parents, teachers, and administrators.

Furthermore, some groups of teachers in the United States are organizing themselves to improve public education for their students. In 1996, the Teacher Union Reform Network (TURN) was formed by concerned teachers and union leaders from both the National Education Association and American Federation of Teachers (Zwaagstra, Clifton, and Long 2007). Notably, TURN has helped negotiate some collective agreements that replace iron-clad seniority provisions with clauses that allow school districts to consider teaching performance when transferring teachers or deciding which teachers to lay off. We think that these are positive developments that deserve support by the public. Unfortunately, TURN's goals are not shared by all American teachers, and there is no similar reform network of teachers in Canada.

RECOMMENDATIONS

Teachers' unions have been very important for teachers, working to ensure that teachers receive reasonable salaries, decent working conditions, and fair treatment by school boards and administrators. No one begrudges unions this vital responsibility.

However, before parents and other members of the public support proposals made by teachers' unions, they must ask what public interest will be served; they cannot simply assume that the interests of their children will be fostered, they must examine carefully the unions' claims, and they cannot be complacent. To teachers, we give essentially the same advice—be cautious in supporting union ambitions. Teachers must consider their own interests in being effective professionals, taking into account the educational needs and interests of students and the responsibilities of parents.

The primary responsibility for the accountability of school systems rests with those who officially govern them. If unions have received too much sway at the expense of the public, then the major responsibility for this lies with state and provincial governments and school boards. Schools are regulated by laws established by the province or state and, sometimes, by the national government, especially in the United States. In fact, every clause in every collective agreement has been agreed to by school boards in negotiation with teachers' unions. Therefore, we urge all levels of government, including local school boards, to ensure that the public interest is foremost in the policies and regulations they enact and ratify.

BIBLIOGRAPHY

Brimelow, Peter. 2003. *The worm in the apple: How the teacher unions are destroying American education.* New York: HarperCollins.
    This book presents a devastating critique of teachers' unions in the United States and shows how they frequently stand in the way of meaningful education reforms.

Greene, Jay P. 2005. *Education myths: What special interest groups want you to believe about our schools—and why it isn't so.* Lanham, MD: Rowman & Littlefield.
An educational researcher debunks a number of education myths that are supported by teachers' unions, such as schools are underfunded, smaller classes result in students doing better, and the results of high-stakes tests are distorted by teaching to the test.

Guppy, Neil, Robert Crocker, Scott Davies, Claire LaPointe, and Larry Sackney. 2005. *Parent and teacher views on education.* Kelowna, BC: Society for the Advancement of Excellence in Education.
This study examines public opinion surveys of teachers and parents and shows that both tend to support such reforms as parental choice of schools, performance-based pay for teachers, and standardized testing of students.

Lawton, Stephen B., George J. Bedard, Duncan K. MacLellan, and Xiaobin Li. 1999. *Teachers' unions in Canada.* Calgary, AB: Detselig.
This book provides a useful overview of the history and status of teachers' unions in Canada.

Litzcke, Karen. 2001. *Teachers unions as players in education reform: A Canadian look at an American trend.* Kelowna, BC: Society for the Advancement of Excellence in Education.
This report describes some educational reforms favored by American teachers' unions and identifies ones that will likely have positive effects on the educational achievement of students.

Weingarten, Randi. 2009. The case for national standards. *Washington Post.* February 16.
This article, written by the president of the American Federation of Teachers, convincingly argues for national standards in curriculum content.

Zwaagstra, Michael, Rodney A. Clifton, and John C. Long. 2007. *Getting the fox out of the schoolhouse: How the public can take back public education.* Halifax, NS: Atlantic Institute for Market Studies.
This monograph examines the impact that teachers' unions have had on educational policies in both Canada and the United States. A number of recommendations in the report advance the public interest in educational reform.

There Is Too Much "Edu-Babble"

It was only the third week of the teacher education program for Elizabeth Oberheimer and she was already feeling overwhelmed. Having recently completed her Bachelor of Science degree, Elizabeth decided that she wanted to become a high school science teacher. So, she enrolled in the after-degree program at the school of education in the local university, which required two years of courses and several weeks of practice teaching. Although she had worked hard and done very well in her science degree, she was finding her education courses challenging in a different way.

Today, in a course called The Foundations of Teaching in the Secondary School, her professor was giving a lecture about teaching strategies. "So, as you can see, combining authentic assessment with holistic, student-centered teaching, in an environment that is conducive to critical thinking, makes for student engagement at a deeper level. Abandoning rote learning in favor of teaching for understanding is the best way of helping your students learn how to learn," explained Professor Jarvis.

As had happened before, Elizabeth didn't have much of a clue what the professor meant. Up went her hand. "Professor Jarvis, could you please clarify your last statement? I'm not sure I understand what you mean, exactly."

"No problem," replied Professor Jarvis. "We know that since all knowledge is ultimately socially constructed by individual learners, content-based curricula are inherently inferior to a learning-to-learn approach. Since all students have different types of intelligences, we have to make sure we adapt our instruction to match their specific needs in a context-rich environment supportive of meaning-making. This is how we help students become lifelong learners. Does that help to clarify things?" asked Professor Jarvis.

Elizabeth still didn't understand what Professor Jarvis meant, but she was not yet confident enough to ask questions when the other students were nodding their heads in agreement. She meekly nodded her head, too, and Professor Jarvis resumed her lecture. It was loaded with more words and phrases that Elizabeth still found incomprehensible after being in the course for three weeks.

After the class was over, Elizabeth caught up with her friend Zeke, who had taken the course the previous year. "When you took this course," began Elizabeth, "could you understand what Professor Jarvis was saying or what she meant? I was really confused again today."

"Don't worry about it," replied Zeke. "Jarvis lectures in ways that make many secondary education students chuckle because what she says often amounts to nonsense. We call it 'edu-babble.' It's just a bunch of words that make education professors feel that they have something important to say. The students in second year think that the professors don't want to be understood too easily by people outside the profession because then their ideas might actually be challenged."

"That sounds weird," replied Elizabeth. "How am I supposed to pass these courses if everything is spoken in a code that I don't understand?"

"The trick is to make sure you memorize the professors' favorite terms and phrases, and that you are prepared to regurgitate them in the reflection papers or personal narratives they assign. Last year, in Jarvis's course, I wrote a reflection paper called 'Gender Disparity in the Teaching of Mathematics.' Everything in the paper was bogus. I made up all the quotes from teachers and parents; I even made up their names and the places where I interviewed them. But, because I used a bunch of concepts from her lectures and paid homage to her ideological perspective, I got an A. Some reflection, I say! You see, most of the professors just want you to adopt their way of thinking, and if you do that, you will be okay," concluded Zeke.

Elizabeth headed off to her next class. As she walked down the hallway, she couldn't decide what disturbed her more—most of her professors using a lot of jargon to explain what seemed to be fairly simple ideas, or that intelligent students like Zeke were so disdainful of some of the professors that they felt it was legitimate to deceive them. She certainly didn't like the idea of submitting a phony assignment, as Zeke did, to succeed in the course.

"I guess it's time for me to start mastering edu-babble, or seriously challenging some of my professors' ideas and advice," said Elizabeth to herself. "I know it is going to be tough, but I really want to be a teacher. I love science, and I really like working with young people. But, dealing with this edu-babble really frustrates me."

INTRODUCTION

Elizabeth is discovering that progressive educational thought is often imbued with jargon, edu-speak, or edu-babble. Many student teachers discover that they can either adopt this way of speaking uncritically or, following Zeke's advice, pretend to adopt it by inserting the educationally correct words and phrases into their discussions and assignments.

It is regrettable when college and university students who want to become teachers think that they must use edu-babble to succeed in their courses. Will any students be inclined to challenge edu-babble, as Elizabeth alone seems prepared to do? It seems to us that not only do student teachers need to deal critically with edu-babble, but so do practicing teachers, school administrators, and parents. Everybody needs to listen carefully to what educators are saying to ensure that they are not intimidated or beguiled by rhetoric.

Of course, people in every profession and occupation use specialized terms to communicate with their colleagues about their work. If you listen to a conversation between two lawyers, for example, you are likely to hear many technical terms that you may not understand. The same is true for dentists, farmers, locomotive engineers, and medical doctors.

In communicating with their occupational fellows, these professionals use a specialized vocabulary because it is precise in expressing specific ideas. People outside the occupation often call this specialized language "jargon" because the words and expressions are not understandable to them, and they perhaps fail to appreciate that the specialized terms and phrases are meaningful to those within the occupational group.

However, according to E. D. Hirsch Jr. (1996) and other critics of edu-babble (see Green 2009 and Ravitch 2007), the jargon used by some educational

theorists and practitioners is quite different. Edu-speak, or edu-babble consists essentially of "seductive rhetorical flourishes [that] pretend to more
soundness, humaneness, substance, and scientific authority than they in fact
possess," says Hirsch (1996, 239).

Such jargon or edu-babble provides the comfort of correctness about educational ideas and practices because a doctrinal consensus is presupposed by
the users. The terms and phrases do not require discussion, and debate is not
necessary. For example, the phrase "child-centered education" is seductive
jargon because simply uttering this phrase implies the approval of what is
everywhere and always good for children in schools; if an educational idea or
practice does not meet some presumed standard of being "child-centered," it
is, by definition, not good for children. When educators use edu-babble, they
are often shielding themselves from a critical examination of the ideas and
practices that the terms apparently represent.

In this chapter, our purpose is to examine a number of terms and expressions commonly used in education that qualify as edu-babble. There are, in
fact, hundreds of these phrases; we examine some of the most outrageous
ones, classifying them into three groups: the good, the bad, and the ugly.
The "good" ones are those that describe educational practices in such a way
that it is almost impossible for anyone to disagree; the "bad" ones are those
that demonize traditional teaching practices; and the "ugly" ones describe
teaching and learning practices that are empty of meaning, bordering on the
nonsensical.

THE GOOD

Virtually all educational ideas that are considered modern, innovative, and
progressive are expressed in ways that make them very difficult to question or
criticize because they are implicitly desirable. "Student-centered" or "child-
centered" education is a very good example of edu-babble, the use of a term that
alone puts its advocates on the side of the angels. Of course, it makes sense for
teachers to consider the needs and interests of students, but this label, by itself,
does not allow us to identify the most effective instructional practices. If being
student-centered means that the needs and interests of students are important
in teaching, then teachers and parents, indeed, everyone, will agree.

Unfortunately, as we have seen, student-centered education often means
using instructional practices that reduce teachers to mere learning facilitators

and encourage students to learn only what they themselves think is worthwhile. The term child-centered is used to validate practices that even many educators might question. We disagree with using student-centered education as a platitude to support only certain teaching practices, and we regret the way the romantic progressive educators have discouraged legitimate debate about its pitfalls.

As well, we hear progressive educators, who want to replace curriculum-based standardized tests with performance checklists and personal narratives, say that the assessment of student learning must be "authentic." This is meant to imply that standardized, multiple-choice tests are not authentic, and, therefore, are inferior because they are not a genuine, reasonable, or appropriate way to assess students' achievement. But in this circular argument, checklists and narratives are apparently genuine, reasonable, and appropriate, and, consequently, are superior assessment devices because they are authentic.

The reality is that authentic assessment is a well-chosen code word for favoring the replacement of standardized, multiple-choice tests with other forms of assessment that often have lower reliability and validity as measures of academic achievement. By using the word "authentic," progressive educators force supporters of standardized, multiple-choice tests into the unenviable position of defending these tests as "inauthentic," though there are good reasons for teachers using all of the various assessment techniques, depending on the characteristics of the students and their instructional objectives. Unfortunately, this argument is difficult to make when standardized tests are implicitly characterized as "inauthentic" and deemed inferior.

No discussion of edu-babble would be complete without mentioning the overused phrase "hands-on learning." If this term means that students should be able to acquire their learning in life-like, direct, even tactile, ways, we agree that this is one way to learn. After all, who would seriously advocate "hands-off" learning, especially when we know, for example, the value of demonstrations, laboratories, and apprenticeships? But, hands-on learning is frequently used to favor project-style methods and to disdain whole-class, direct instruction or lecturing as being too verbal or abstract.

For students, project methods, especially discovery learning, may be interesting, and perhaps fun, but they are often inefficient, uncertain in their instructional outcomes, and unfair because not all students can learn in this way. Also, not every subject or idea can be learned well by hands-on projects.

For example, it is defensible to teach basic arithmetic in the early grades with marbles, but there are topics, even in the elementary school curriculum, that are abstract and cannot be taught using concrete things. Effective teachers know that hands-on learning has specific limitations where abstract ideas must be taught, and they resist assuming that hands-on is the only or best way to learn.

"Critical-thinking skills" and "higher-order thinking" are obviously important instructional objectives. To say that students should learn to think critically and at a higher level are virtually nondebatable teaching aims, though it is not so easy to identify the specific teaching and learning techniques that will produce these outcomes reliably.

However, it is debatable when these terms are used to de-emphasize or trivialize the knowing of facts, focusing on the nebulous idea that students can think critically without having an extensive amount of sound factual knowledge. For example, it is impossible to think critically about astronomy with little understanding of mathematics and physics. That is, critical thinking is not simply a matter of having certain procedural skills or the ability to express strong opinions readily. Too often, progressive educators counterpoise critical thinking with the learning of "mere facts," as if they are opposites. Clearly, they are not. While we agree that students should learn to think critically, common sense tells us that they need to know some things reasonably well before they can think critically about them.

THE BAD

There is no shortage of pejorative or disparaging terms that have been coined to discredit traditional approaches to teaching and learning. Consequently, it is not surprising that many traditional practices have fallen out of favor, and that many parents and citizens feel at a loss when they listen to, or try to talk to, so-called educational experts. For example, "rote learning" is almost always used to connote a negative educational activity.

At one time, it was considered valuable for students to learn to spell words correctly, to practice their printing and writing, and to memorize the multiplication tables, which are all forms of rote learning. Now, teachers who use rote learning to help their students master foundational knowledge and skills are criticized for being old-fashioned. This is discouraging to some teachers. After all, who wants to be a boring teacher who forces students to memorize facts and practice fundamental skills at the expense of engaging them in critical thinking?

If discrediting rote learning is insufficient to intimidate and annoy teachers and parents, "drill and kill" will certainly do the trick. Teachers who have their students master basic skills by frequent repetition and recitation—drill—are apparently taking away the joy that students have in discovering things on their own. However, most skills in life need to be practiced if they are going to be mastered. Think of the sports coach who tells her players that "you play the way you practice." To that coach, practicing drills is strongly related to playing the game well, which the players also know is true.

Indeed, players often say that they enjoy their practice sessions because they are improving their skills. However, to describe similar teaching strategies in schools as "drill and kill" is a terrible condemnation. No wonder many teachers are reluctant to do anything that might earn them membership in the club that "drills and kills" students.

Another epithet that is often hurled at schools or classrooms where a mandated curriculum, direct instruction, and formal testing are routine is that they are "factory-model schools." We concede that schools are bureaucratic organizations which must carry out important routine tasks with large numbers of students and teachers, even restricting their freedom.

But, this does not make schools into factories. As Hirsch (1996, 252) observes: "What is really at stake . . . is the association of the factory model with 'traditional pedagogy,' as though the two were indissolubly wedded." The association is entirely polemical in that it is claimed that traditional educational methods are the cause of factory-model schools; it is also a grossly unfair stereotype of both students and teachers who are simply engaged in the necessary task of schooling. Who seriously favors treating children as passive entities on an assembly line, progressing uniformly, with authoritarian teachers who perform repetitive tasks with insufficient humanity and little creativity? Were there any such schools, we, too, would abhor them; but this kind of exaggeration is neither fair nor useful in the difficult task of improving schools.

THE UGLY

Some of the worst examples of edu-babble are truly ugly—empty of meaning, bordering on the nonsensical. "Less is more" is a popular term for progressives; it is used to justify the notion that when teachers focus on fewer topics then students learn more. Many people will probably be suspicious of the inherent contradiction in this statement, which seems to make about as much sense as "nothing is everything." The claim is that having less academic content and fewer topics makes it possible for students to gain a deeper understanding of the subject matter.

In contrast, the commonsense idea is that "less is really less" and "more is really more." When academic content is reduced, students learn less than they would if more content were studied. We concede that a gain in depth is one possible consequence of reducing breadth, but this outcome is not guaranteed by the label "less is more." How much breadth and how much depth to give a subject area or particular topics within a subject area is a major question of curriculum design and delivery. As such, it is a real dilemma that curriculum guides and teacher education programs are intended to help resolve. And the metaphor "less is more" is unhelpful to serious teachers and concerned parents who are trying to ensure that children are well educated.

Another popular phrase we often hear from educators is that education is essentially "meaning-making in a context-rich environment." Apparently, this phrase is a description of the teaching-learning process, in its essence, and the typical school environment that supports it. Progressives use this phrase to promote teaching practices and classroom organization and procedures that favor students constructing their own understandings rather than those that experts have already achieved. On this notion, students determine their own meanings and teachers are present to ensure that the educational environment supports their independence.

This implies that teachers are there not so much to teach subjects as to create educational environments that support students in developing their own understandings. However, it is almost impossible for students to discover, on their own, the principles of calculus or harmony, for example. These discoveries were acts of genius and the product of centuries of thought and study. In this instance, the progressives are confusing how the discovery was made, or how the idea developed, with the way that students can best understand it.

Most students will never independently rediscover the mathematical principles of calculus that took Leibniz and Newton years to develop no matter how "context-rich" their environment is. Besides, it is a waste of time because mathematicians have already discovered the fundamental principles. Common sense tells us that students should study and apply the fundamental principles that have already been identified and refined by experts before they try to discover any principles of calculus naively, uncritically, or without understanding how such principles came to be accepted. Of course, students who are earnest to learn benefit from surroundings rich in inspiration and support. But, surely, a very important part of that treasured environment is the richness of competent and astute teachers who not only inspire and support their students, but who also plan, instruct, and evaluate.

A final example of ugly edu-babble is the assertion by educators that their students are "learning to learn." Sometimes parents become so baffled by terms like this that they do not ask the educators to define them for fear that they will be considered ignorant. For progressives, learning to learn justifies teachers focusing on the process of learning and the skills of investigation; that is, knowing how to find information is more important than knowing specific information, especially if it is unrelated, isolated facts. The basic argument is that because many facts eventually become outdated, students should not learn useless information. However, when this idea means that teachers pay little or no attention to specific information, it is problematic.

First, not all factual information is useless; some of it is useful for a long period of time; indeed, it contributes significantly to what is called our current understanding. Second, because we cannot be certain what factual information will have permanence, students need to know how to find new information that is relevant to their current understanding. Finally, students need to see if their current understanding should be modified in the light of the new information; that is, to use the new information to think critically and imaginatively about their new understanding while disregarding what is no longer salient.

It is impossible to think in this way without using inferences, reasoning, and sometimes, recognizing the specific facts that support general principles. When progressives advocate that "learning-to-learn" skills are so superior that they eliminate the necessity for acquiring factual knowledge, their counsel is seriously inadequate, if not foolish. It makes about as much sense as "swimming to swim" without any water.

RECOMMENDATIONS

Edu-babble seems to have the highest currency among educational reformers, or gurus, and professors of education. According to E. D. Hirsch Jr. (1996), these people have the major responsibility for interpreting a relatively straightforward activity—teaching children in schools—as unnecessarily complex by using numerous faddish terms and phrases that we have characterized as edu-babble, good, bad, and ugly. Most worrisome is that uniniti-ated student teachers and parents can be intimidated and confused by those who use an esoteric vocabulary that apparently only experts can understand. Consequently, we plead with our fellow educators, especially professors, not to use edu-babble; rather, we ask them to explain their ideas in terms that are precise, even technical, but made meaningful to their audience.

Our advice to parents and student teachers is similar: don't be intimidated by edu-babblers. If some educational ideas seem incomprehensible to you, ask the speaker for explanations in precise and meaningful language. In ad-dition, use your intelligence and common sense, but also be prepared to do some reading on your own to become familiar with educational ideas. And when you are talking with educators, give them the same courtesy you expect by using plain language yourself.

Let us all make a sustained effort to stamp out edu-babble. Incompre-hensible expressions and esoteric terms are not badges of professionalism or high regard for educators. It is certainly time to ensure that clarity, integrity, and dignified debate characterize discussions of education and the important work of schools.

BIBLIOGRAPHY

Fosnot, Catherine, ed. 2005. *Constructivism: Theory, perspectives, and practice.* New York: Teachers College Press.
    This book is edited by one of the foremost proponents of constructivism. Some readers will be challenged to know exactly what the writers mean in some of the contributions because of the use of expressions that amount to edu-babble.

Green, Gwendolyn. 2009. *Edu-babble: The glamorous world of the New York City public school system.* New York: Author Solutions.
    The book identifies a number of terms used by educators in New York City that the author considers edu-babble.

Hirsch, E. D., Jr. 1996. *The schools we need and why we don't have them.* New York: Doubleday.
    In a very informative appendix, Hirsch presents the definitions of almost sixty of the most common edu-babble words and phrases used by the progressives.

Kramer, Rita. 1991. *Ed school follies: The miseducation of America's teachers.* New York: The Free Press.
Kramer is a well-known journalist who spent a year visiting schools of education throughout the United States. She exposes some of the educational doublespeak that student teachers encounter from professors of education.

Nikiforuk, Andrew. 1994. *If learning is so natural, why am I going to school? A parent's guide.* Toronto, ON: Penguin Books.
This is a dictionary of seventy-five educational ideas and terms that were commonly used in Canada in the early 1990s; many are still in use.

Perlstein, Linda. 2004. Talking the edutalk: Jargon becoming prevalent in the classroom. *Washington Post.* January 18.
This article provides a number of examples of edu-babble that are used to keep parents misinformed about what is happening in classrooms.

Ravitch, Diane. 2007. *EdSpeak: A glossary of education terms, phrases, buzzwords, and jargon.* Alexandria, VA: Association for Supervision and Curriculum Development.
This monograph provides a valuable resource that translates over five hundred examples of educational jargon, much of it edu-babble, into everyday English.

Conclusion

Using Common Sense to Obtain Better Schools

If you have children in school, perhaps you have experienced one or two of the problems we have discussed and perhaps you have felt uneasy. Perhaps you wanted to ask questions of school officials but didn't feel comfortable doing so because you were somewhat intimidated. Perhaps you have been surprised at some of the policies and practices of North American schools. And you probably realize that there is a deeper struggle—really a war of ideas—going on for the allegiance of educators, parents, and other citizens regarding the appropriate education of children.

One approach to public education, the perspective of the romantic progressives, has the substantial allegiance of many educators, especially those who are responsible for the education of teachers. As supporters of a more traditional and pragmatic approach to education, we think that this trend is lamentable and needs to be challenged. If parents, educators, and other citizens agree with our arguments and proposals, they need to become more vocal and better organized; indeed, they need to be politically active to ensure that all children obtain the education they need and deserve. And we think that our idea of common sense should guide this endeavor.

Why should our notion of common sense guide the effort to improve public education? The short answer is that too many current policies and practices in schools reflect the abandonment of common sense. The wisdom of practical experience and tradition too often have been trivialized or dismissed by the romantic progressives. Perhaps with the best of intentions, the progressives have allowed their enthusiasm for certain policies and practices to exceed the limitations of their evidence, and have allowed their ideology to overtake caution when it comes to the limitations of educational theory and research. In short, the superiority of their approach has not been adequately justified.

We have endeavored to offer a counterpoint of common sense and pragmatism to what we consider are mistaken ideas and unwise prescriptions that we think have weakened public education and public regard for it. But the misdirection of the romantics can be challenged; it is not too late to raise an alarm, and educators, parents, and citizens alike can ring the bell if they act together with common cause and common sense to improve the education of all children.

For those who are motivated to move in a corrective direction, it is encouraging to notice that there are important allies who are helpful in identifying the common ground of effective school reform, even though their focus is somewhat different from ours. Certainly, William Bennett, Chester Finn Jr., and John Cribb Jr. (1999); Jay P. Greene (2005); E. D. Hirsch Jr. (1996); Mark Holmes (1998); and Diane Ravitch (2000) are allies. But the works of E. D. Hirsch Jr. (1996) and Jay P. Greene (2005) are especially noteworthy.

As noted earlier, Hirsch's contribution is significant for educators, parents, and public policymakers. In *The Schools We Need and Why We Don't Have Them*, Hirsch (1996, 237) makes a fundamental observation that undergirds our call for concerted action that will promote better public schools:

> It has taken nearly seventy years for Romantic progressivism to exercise . . . intellectual dominion over not just schools of education but a large percentage of policymakers and the general public as well. Nothing truly effective in the way of large scale policy change . . . can be accomplished . . . until there is a change of mind by the general public—among whom I include . . . teachers.

For us as for Hirsch (1996, 230), a number of faculty members in schools of education must bear some responsibility for the undesirable predicament of many North American public schools:

> Education schools currently do not convey to our teachers the results of . . . firmly established research showing the superior effectiveness of clear focus, definite standards, diligent practice, and continual monitoring through tests

and other means. Instead . . . education schools derogate such traditional practices in favor of the progressive program of individual pacing, discovery learning, thematic teaching, non-objective testing, and so on . . . which are, indeed, presented as fruits of the most recent research. The resulting pandemic of mistaken ideas may be the gravest barrier to . . . educational improvement.

Hirsch's critique may be too scathing in scope, especially given the diversity of views evident in most schools of education, but he is correct in identifying one significant source of the ideology of romantic progressivism.

Consistent with the most reputable research on effective schools (see Marzano 2003; Ouchi 2003), Hirsch (1996, 237) favors an individual "school-by-school grassroots effort" that can be supported by a number of larger-scale initiatives, such as greater parental choice, "which give parents and teachers the power to change their own individual schools, so long as their students are trained to high standards of skill and knowledge."

This requirement of Hirsch is the core of his advocacy, and is discerning for those who think that public schools in both Canada and the United States need rescue:

> The possible administrative means for accomplishing the task are many, but there can be no substitute for the main elements of the task itself. Schools need to have a coherent, cumulative core curriculum which instills consensus values such as civic duty, honesty, diligence, perseverance, respect, kindness, and independent-mindedness; which gives students step-by-step mastery of *procedural knowledge* in language arts and mathematics; which gives them step-by-step mastery of *content knowledge* in civics, science, the arts, and the humanities; and which holds students, teachers, schools, and parents accountable for acceptable progress in achieving these specific year-by-year goals. (Hirsch 1996, 236)

A recent book by Jay Greene (2005), *Education Myths: What Special Interest Groups Want You to Believe about Our Schools—and Why It Isn't So*, is also inspiring to those of us who are looking for ways to obtain better public schools. Essentially, Greene (2005, 1) says that myths—"beliefs that people adopt because they have an air of plausibility, people want to believe they're true, and . . . are consistent with at least some pieces of evidence"—dominate educational policy. Though myths are at best only partial truths, they nevertheless "cause us to misunderstand the nature of the problems in our schools, to continue engaging in practices that shortchange students, and to resist the adoption of effective reforms that would improve education" (Greene 2005, 2).

Greene, in fact, identifies eighteen myths about public education and dispels them all with compelling evidence and forceful arguments. For example, he debunks the myths that accountability is an expensive and unwise intervention for schools and that school choice accelerates racial segregation. Greene (2005, 2) contends that for public schools to be improved, we must find ways to dispel the myths that stand in the way of progress because "we wouldn't think that schools fail because they lack adequate resources, we wouldn't continue paying ineffective teachers the same as effective ones, and we would support proven reforms like accountability and school choice" if we didn't cling to these myths.

Furthermore, Greene (2005, 220) adds, we must confront the falsehood that schools are to be protected from the use of incentives:

> The power of incentives to change behavior, and therefore to improve outcomes when properly harnessed and to harm outcomes when improperly aligned, is a pattern that emerges across the whole body of evidence in education. Adding resources without changing incentives doesn't work. Imposing accountability incentives through positive and negative consequences for performance works. Providing incentives through choice, ensuring that schools . . . compete for students by offering more effective . . . services, also works.

In the choice of policies for improving schools, Greene warns against showing any special deference to educational insiders: "Educational practitioners, such as teachers, school administrators, and especially professors at education schools, are not necessarily reliable judges of an education policy's merits. . . . [W]e should be careful not to treat their claims as though they were comprehensive assessments made by neutral experts" (Greene 2005, 3).

Readers will recognize that, although we are "education insiders," our critique of public schooling and our proposals for strengthening it resonate strongly with the writings of both Hirsch and Greene. In short, our commonsense perspective calls for confronting the rising tide of romantic progressivism because of its misdirection of educational aims and methods. Moreover, we note that some of the beliefs that the romantic progressives and their followers find comforting are the very myths that Greene has exposed. Along with Hirsch and Greene, we believe that better public schools are not possible until we improve their accountability and use appropriate incentives to encourage specific improvements. Investing more money and creating more regulations will not work; effective accountability and appropriate incentives are more likely to work.

However, improving public education will not be accomplished without significant engagement of the citizenry. In this respect, citizens, including sympathetic educators, must take politically astute, grassroots action that promotes the reshaping of education policy and practice. No one who favors better schools or takes seriously our arguments and proposals can be complacent. An intelligent skepticism of educational ideas and practices, that reflects our notion of common sense, can counter complacency.

But teachers, administrators, parents, indeed all citizens should be prepared to challenge the educational establishment if it marginalizes their concerns or restricts the effective expression of them. Otherwise, we risk continuing to be beguiled by the myths and mistaken ideas that prevent public schools from making even the modest changes that could improve the educational success of many children.

Of course, we recognize that there is variation among schools regarding the policies and practices they favor. Some teachers and school administrators have adopted a progressive ideology to a much greater degree than others, and there are educators who are sympathetic to our critique and already have implemented recommendations similar to the ones we make; still others may be inclined to adopt some of our recommendations. As a result, our criticisms are less applicable to some schools, school jurisdictions, and schools of education than to others. In fact, there are many excellent teachers, administrators, school board members, and professors who are working diligently under trying circumstances. We want to support those who think, for example, that subject matter still matters in schools, and that teaching it well and testing properly for its mastery are worthy professional responsibilities.

If your children happen to have excellent teachers and excellent schools, make sure that you tell the teachers, the administrators, the school board, and other people that you are pleased. If you happen to work as an educator in such schools, then tell other educators and parents the basis for the success you and your colleagues experience. If you are a student teacher, and you have some professors who explain why direct teaching and practice are important, testing is essential, and that you have an obligation to tell parents plainly how well their children are doing, make sure that you tell your professors that you appreciate their advice.

The fact that research and scholarship in education is not definitive means that by now you know it is inappropriate for experts to claim that "the research proves that teachers and administrators should do such-and-such." At best, research suggests that doing one thing is generally more effective than doing something else. No research study dictates exactly what teachers and administrators should do with the unique group of students in their classrooms and schools. Sometimes small reforms will be enough, and they do not necessarily require the specific support of large scale initiatives. Obviously, we do not expect readers to agree with everything that we recommend, but we hope that you will see that our advice is based on common sense, research evidence, and argumentation.

Finally, we summarize the major recommendations that are made in the book. They are numbered to indicate where they are mainly discussed; for example, recommendations 1.1 to 1.4 are presented in chapter 1, and recommendations 2.1, 2.2, and 2.3 are from chapter 2, and so on.

1.1 Overall, public schooling should provide the means and the opportunity for the development of the individual's talents in the balanced pursuit of the good life.

1.2 The curriculum of the public school should emphasize academic content that prepares students for a successful livelihood and the responsibilities of democratic citizenship.

1.3 Virtually all students, at every grade level, should be required to demonstrate a substantial proficiency in the knowledge and skills of a core curriculum so that they can read, write, and use basic mathematics competently, and, on graduation from high school, they are familiar with the important ideas and achievements in the sciences, literature, and the arts, and have an understanding of at least their nation's history, social institutions, and government.

1.4 The core curriculum should be mandated by the state or province and should be viable within assured instructional time requirements.

2.1 Both classroom-based assessments and standardized tests should be an integral part of teaching and learning in public schools.

2.2 A regular and formal testing regime, including standardized tests, should be used in public schools, especially at the middle and high school levels.

2.3   Institutions of teacher education should teach prospective teachers how to use a wide repertoire of techniques for assessing students' achievements.

3.1   All schools should establish clear behavioral expectations for students, communicate them to parents and the community, and ensure that they are consistently enforced with specific consequences.

3.2   Persistently unruly students should not be allowed to jeopardize the safety and education of other students.

4.1   The principle of inclusivity should not be used to place all children, regardless of ability, performance, and needs, in regular classrooms.

4.2   For students who require specialized instruction, support, and care, the principle of accommodation to their ability, performance, and needs should be considered in deciding the school placement that is most advantageous to them.

4.3   School jurisdictions and schools should give more attention in programming and instruction to the abilities, needs, and interests of children who are gifted.

5.1   School jurisdictions should establish and maintain a systematic scheme for assessing teaching and administrative effectiveness, and they should use performance-based awards to recognize meritorious performance.

5.2   School jurisdictions should provide expanded opportunities for outstanding educators to mentor others.

6.1   School boards should ensure that their schools are effective and accountable to parents and citizens, especially in respect of the provision of timely and reliable information about the success of the students.

6.2   School administrators should have significant decision-making authority in creating and sustaining effective schools.

6.3   Because principals perform the essential managerial role in schools, they should not be members of the teachers' bargaining unit or union.

6.4   School boards should provide parents with greater choice of schools for the education of their children.

7.1   Teachers should have the right and responsibility to orchestrate their students' learning, subject to the requirements of the mandated curriculum and the effectiveness of their pedagogical choices.

8.1   Teachers should recognize that direct teaching is an effective instructional technique, especially for struggling students.

9.1 Teachers should recognize that rote learning and sustained practice are beneficial to students' learning.

10.1 Students should be expected to complete a reasonable amount of homework that promotes their achievement of the instructional objectives.

10.2 School boards should not unreasonably constrain teachers' discretion in the assignment of homework.

11.1 Grading schemes should evaluate students' achievements in ways that are meaningful to the students and parents so that their success and the basis for improvement are clear.

12.1 School boards should ensure that specific achievement standards of knowledge and skill govern the promotion of students.

13.1 Parents and other citizens should be skeptical of the claims by teachers' unions that they act in the best interests of students.

13.2 All levels of government, including local school boards, should ensure that the public interest is foremost in the policies and regulations they enact.

14.1 Mystifying educational jargon or edu-babble should be discarded in favor of clear and precise terminology.

BIBLIOGRAPHY

Bennett, William. J., Chester E. Finn Jr., and John T. E. Cribb Jr. 1999. *The educated child: A parent's guide from preschool through eighth grade.* New York: The Free Press. This book challenges the mediocrity found in many American public schools and identifies the core curriculum all children should master at each grade.

Greene, Jay P. 2005. *Education myths: What special-interest groups want you to believe about our schools—And why it isn't so.* Lanham, MD: Rowman & Littlefield. Greene effectively debunks a number of education myths that dominate educational policy in both Canada and the United States. He argues that these myths are, at best, only partial truths that account for the substantial resistance to educational reforms.

Hirsch, E. D., Jr. 1996. *The schools we need and why we don't have them.* New York: Doubleday. In this book, educational critic and reformer E. D. Hirsch Jr. effectively counters the ideas and practices of the romantic progressives that he sees as obstacles to obtaining better schools.

Holmes, Mark. 1998. *The reformation of Canada's schools: Breaking the barriers to parental choice.* Kingston, ON: McGill-Queen's University Press.
A retired school administrator and former professor of education at the Ontario Institute for Studies in Education, University of Toronto, argues vigorously against the dominant progressive mind-set and in favor of more traditional approaches to education. Because parents are not likely to agree on the goals of schools, he argues that parents need to have choices in the public schools their children attend.

Marzano, Robert J. 2003. *What works in schools: Translating research into action.* Alexandria, VA: Association for Supervision and Curriculum Development.
The author argues that if we follow the guidance arising from the most reputable educational research, we can achieve unprecedented effectiveness in public education.

Ouchi, William G. 2003. *Making schools work: A revolutionary plan to get your children the education they need.* New York: Simon & Schuster.
This book shows how effective schools work and identifies the strategies that committed and skillful school administrators use to improve the academic performances of their students.

Ravitch, Diane. 2000. *Left back: A century of failed school reforms.* New York: Simon & Schuster.
Former United States assistant secretary of education Diane Ravitch shows how the romantic progressive ideology has damaged public education in the United States.

About the Authors

Michael C. Zwaagstra has more than a decade of teaching experience at a variety of grade levels and currently teaches high school social studies at Green Valley School in Manitoba. He is also a research associate with the Frontier Centre for Public Policy (fcpp.org) who specializes in education policy. He received his BEd, PBCE, and MEd degrees from the University of Manitoba, where his academic awards included the A. W. Hogg Undergraduate Scholarship, the Klieforth Prize in American History, the Aaron Bricker Memorial Scholarship, and the Schoolmasters' Wives Association Scholarship. His columns promoting commonsense education reform have been published in major daily newspapers such as the *National Post, Calgary Herald, Winnipeg Free Press,* and *Saskatoon StarPhoenix.*

Rodney A. Clifton has a BEd and an MEd from the University of Alberta, a PhD from the University of Toronto, and a fil. dr. from the University of Stockholm. He is a professor in the Faculty of Education at the University of Manitoba and, over the past thirty-three years, has published numerous articles, monographs, and books. Rod Clifton has also received a Spencer Fellowship from the International Association for the Evaluation of Educational Achievement, an Rh Award from the University of Manitoba, a R. W. B. Jackson Research Award from the Canadian Educational Researchers' Association, and both an Edward Sheffield Award and a Distinguished Research Award from the Canadian Society for the Study of Higher Education.

John C. Long has a BEd from the University of Alberta, an MEd from the University of Calgary, and a PhD from the University of Alberta. He was a professor of educational administration at the University of Manitoba until his retirement in 2008, and currently holds an appointment as senior scholar at the university. His professional background includes work as a certified teacher, school administrator, and university staff-relations officer. His research interest in educational policy, politics, and law has focused recently on the impact of Charter-inspired litigation on Canadian school systems. Among his recent publications are "Canadian Pluralism, the Charter and Citizenship Education" (with R. Magsino and R. Theberge), in *Educating Citizens for a Pluralistic Society* (2001); "Encouraging Spirituality: Constraints and Opportunities," in *Inspiring Practice: Spirituality and Educational Leadership* (2005); and "Religion in Canadian Education: Whither Goest Thou?" (with R. Magsino), in *The Courts, the Charter and the Schools* (2010).